## *What others are saying abou*

This beautifully written memoir is a cautionary tale, but it's also a story of redemption and hope for all of us trying to live as Christians in a world where false gods are still alive and well.

Gary Krause,
**director of Adventist Mission**
**author, *God's Great Missionaries***

Andy Nash's latest work *Paper God* is without question his best. It is riveting, penetrating, and deeply personal. His transparency in describing his personal failings is a breath of fresh air. There is true transformation of his heart and yet he leaves us fully aware that he is a man still in process. There were times when I was moved to tears.

Bernie Anderson,
**author of *Breaking the Silence***

# Paper GOD

## Other Books by Andy Nash

*Tatum and Her Tiger: For Kids Blessed With Passion*

*Unleash the Dream*

# Paper GOD

## Stumbling Through Failure to a Deeper Faith

Andy Nash

Pacific Press® Publishing Association
Nampa, Idaho
Oshawa, Ontario, Canada
www.pacificpress.com

Cover design by Steve Lanto
Cover design resources from istockphoto.com
Inside design by Aaron Troia





The author assumes full responsibility for the accuracy of all facts and quotations as cited in this book.

You can obtain additional copies of this book by calling toll-free 1-800-765-6955 or by visiting www.adventistbookcenter.com.

Library of Congress Cataloging-in-Publication Data:

Nash, Andy, 1971-
Paper God : stumbling through failure to a deeper faith / Andy Nash.
p. cm.
ISBN 13: 978-0-8163-2384-5 (pbk.)
ISBN 10: 0-8163-2384-4 (pbk.)
1. Nash, Andy, 1971- 2. Seventh-day Adventists—United States—Biography.
I. Title.
BX6193.N37A3 2010
286.7'32092—dc22
[B]

2009053900

10 11 12 13 14 • 5 4 3 2 1

# Author's Note

This memoir is about a formative period in my life, personally and professionally. As a journalist I care about accuracy and have done my best to verify everything in this book, including facts, dates, and sequences. In some cases, I have changed names but never circumstances. With respect to dialogue, while I'm confident that I recall the wording of most conversations, I've left out quotation marks. Finally, I've written this experience primarily from the limited perspective—what I knew at the time, rather than what I know now. This seems appropriate. If I'd known at the time what I know now, much of this would never have happened.

# Contents

# Preface

As it turns out, the "coolest man on the planet" isn't fulfilled either. Simon Cowell, the admired costar of *American Idol* and *Britain's Got Talent,* says that he often feels empty. "You can be having the best time of your life, and yet you're utterly and totally miserable," he tells London's *Daily Mail.*

In the morning, Simon climbs into his bathtub and watches old *Flintstones* cartoons. "I know it sounds a bit strange," he says about his preference for old cartoons rather than modern ones. "Maybe it reminds me of when I was a kid."

Simon's new fourteen thousand-square-foot Beverly Hills home includes a cinema, a spa, a pool, and a garage in which he parks his Bugatti, Rolls-Royce, Bentley Azure, and Ferrari. None of it makes any lasting difference. "I'm just a wandering asteroid without a home," he says. "I get to points in my life where I sometimes think I'm never going to be happy."

How many of us could say the same?

With both hands, we reach for the debris-filled streams of the world, scooping up more digital channels and cell phone apps and vacation itineraries, and for a while these help us feel better, but then our underlying emptiness and anxiety cry out again, and we reach for more and more and more. We drink deeply from these streams, but eventually they run dry, and still we aren't fulfilled.

So we turn and gaze at those who, like Simon, seem fulfilled—the celebrities and sports stars and other beautiful people who dutifully accompany us through the checkout line. And we think, *Hey, maybe it* is *possible.* Maybe we, too, can attain this level of apparent joy. Buying the myth of "never give up on your dreams," we aim ourselves at impossible targets, sacrificing everything and everyone—*no, not right now, sweetheart*—to get where we think we want to be.

This pursuit of happiness is doubly tragic for those of us who profess faith in God. We open our Scriptures and shake our heads at how the ancients possibly could have worshiped idols of wood and stone—*what were they thinking?*—not bothering to unearth the actual reason: because they made them. We don't want to recognize the strong resemblance of their idols to our own: how we also kneel and bow before them, hoping, praying, that they will somehow make us happy. The worst feeling of all is when we look up and see our own image reflected.

Amazingly, we're willing to take risks in other areas of life but not in the realm of faith. It's only when everything else disappoints us—however long that may take, and often it's a lifetime—that we're willing to reconsider the call of Christ Himself, "He who loses his life . . . will find it" (Matthew 10:39, NKJV). Some do heed this call and testify to how full their lives have become. Often these stories are told by the same people who once accompanied us through the checkout line, the faces that everyone recognizes. They tell how they just reached a place where they knew they had to die to self, and how, by dying, they discovered how to live.

But they aren't the only ones. The millions of ordinary people who share this planet don't feel the cosmic battle for the soul any less powerfully than those in the starlight. We, too, have a story to tell. This, indeed, is the wonder of those whom Christ surrounded Himself with. To build His kingdom, He didn't look to other kings but to the ordinary people who walked the same parched roads. We can take heart that the second most-developed story in the Gospels, behind that of Jesus Himself, is that of another Simon: a common laborer called Simon, son of John—Simon Johnson—who finally let go of all that constrained him and reached, with both hands, for the Living Water.

It's for the other Simon Johnsons out there that I share my own story of faith, failure, and ultimately redemption. I invite you to share your own.

Andy Nash
www.tabgha.org

# Prologue

I needed to come here.

I'm at the lake on a calm spring morning. I'm up to my knees in the water, and some of the rocks hurt my feet, but I absolutely don't mind because this is about the happiest I've felt in my life.

I wasn't prepared for how hard this experience would be, how much it would take out of me. But when you've been sifted and charred, you appreciate simple joy all the more. When you've been through the fire, a walk in the water feels pretty good.

I don't think you can understand the hollowness of a broken dream unless you've experienced it yourself. To join this club, you've got to have a certain look in your eyes—a look of resignation, of exhaustion—a look that says your plans just didn't work out like you thought they would. But it can also be a look of strange serenity, of submission, of finally releasing what you held on to so fiercely.

I didn't fully understand this look in others until I saw it in myself. I didn't know the humiliation until I was knocked flat and forced to acknowledge defeat.

I needed to come here too.

# *Chapter 1* Restless

Seven years and seven months ago, I was spinning restlessly in my office chair. Back and forth I spun.

Shortly, I'd be heading down two flights of stairs to teach the class that every college student takes—freshman composition. My lesson plan lay on my desk; it was the same as last year's. Once you've taught a class such as composition, you're pretty much set. You stand at your lectern, smiling politely as your students file into class, a few of them slowing for a quick question: Did I use this comma correctly here? How long should our essays be again? Then you wait for everyone's attention. OK, you say, let's hear your topics for your descriptive piece. Lauren, we'll start with you. What did you decide is your favorite place in the world?

I spun some more. Then I stopped, unable to escape the truth: I was bored.

This was only my second year as a college professor, and already I was losing interest. I thought I'd done the good family thing here. At the age of twenty-eight I'd left behind a hectic but stimulating editorial job outside Washington, D.C., to take a job teaching English and Communication at Union College in Lincoln, Nebraska. I wanted a safe, affordable place for Cindy and me to raise our two little girls, Ally and Morgan. And I thought that my new schedule would be great for our family: flexible days, holiday breaks, and summers off.

And my schedule was great. Most days I'd come home to eat lunch with Cindy and the girls and hear that morning's big news: a cocoon they'd found, or a new friend they'd met down the street. The other day I'd walked in to see Cindy mockingly pounding her head against the kitchen wall, laughing hysterically.

I'm such a total idiot! she said.

What happened? I asked.

Cindy said that she'd just left a phone message with Pam, a woman in town who had offered us a free kitten. For the past few days, Cindy had been debating whether we should accept the kitten. The girls were only three and one, and Cindy already felt as if she were herding cats. After carefully considering it—even praying about it—Cindy decided it just wasn't the right time for a kitten.

So I call Pam, Cindy said, and leave a message. I say, Hi, Pam, this is Cindy Nash. I'm just calling to thank you for the offer of a free kitten. We really thought long and hard about this, but with the girls still so young, I just decided that I'm not up to a kitten right now. I really hope that you can find a good home for the kitten. In Jesus' name, amen.

I laughed. You really said that? I asked. In Jesus' name, amen?

Yes! Cindy screamed. How could I do that?

So then what did you do?

Well, I just paused a second, and then I said, Um, this is still Cindy here. I'm not sure why I just said in Jesus' name, amen. But I hope you find a good home for the kitten. Bye.

She fell against me, laughing. This was classic Cindy—the girl I'd fallen in love with so quickly when she'd suddenly appeared, a new nursing student, my senior year of college. So beautiful and so real. I loved that I had married her, loved how she loved our girls, and loved our life together. I couldn't have planned it any better.

The only thing I hadn't planned was how I was feeling at work—how teaching left me empty. It wasn't that I didn't enjoy my students. I liked them a lot, and apparently they liked me too. I just didn't like repeating the same material over and over.

Earlier in the semester I talked with one of my colleagues, Chris Blake, over lunch, about the sinking feeling that I was in the wrong field.

Don't you get bored teaching the same material year after year? I asked.

I don't teach material, Chris said. I teach people.

Yes, of course. What Chris said made sense. Intellectually, I recognized the distinction right away. When you teach people, the experience is always new. People are always different, so the experience is always different. This was a helpful perspective, and I hoped that it would work for me.

* * * * *

OK, Nancy, let's move on to you. Tell us about your favorite place.

Nancy's favorite place in the world is sitting on the roof of her barn back home. She's especially nostalgic for her barn, since she's away from home for the first time. Nancy's barn is a great topic really—much different from the usual favorite places students list off: Grandma's kitchen, an amusement park, their room. The roof of a barn is a cool idea for a favorite place in the world.

OK, I say, what specifically do you enjoy about sitting on the roof of your barn? I'm trying to help Nancy develop her supporting ideas.

Well, she says, it's just so quiet up there, and I have a chance to think.

OK, good, so one of your points is the quiet—the solitude. No noise, right? No TV, no traffic, no teachers asking about topics. We laugh.

I do get pleasure in these moments. They flicker like the evening fireflies at Nancy's barn. For brief moments I'm happy, but they never last. I don't want to feel this way, but I do. How can you keep yourself from waking up in the morning with the lingering sense that you're just not happy? How can you make that go away?

I heard once that each of us looks for fulfillment in one of three areas.

Some of us look to possessions—what we have.

Others of us look to people—relationships, socializing, and popularity.

Still others look to performance—what we accomplish.

That was definitely me: fulfillment through performance. I viewed my performance as an extension of myself. If I were working on a project, that project became part of me. In fact, I cared more what people thought of my work than what people thought of me. My work was me.

* * * * *

I looked at my watch—still plenty of time before class. I reached for the Bible on my desk and spun my chair to my outside window. Since the start of the school year, I had been reading through the book of John, and today I was on the final chapter, John 21. I knew this story well.

After the crucifixion and resurrection of Jesus, Peter and the other disciples had returned to the north shore of the Sea of Galilee, where Peter had lived and worked as a fisherman for most of his life. Unexpectedly, Jesus met them there, miraculously filling their empty nets, just as He'd done three years earlier. As the nets burst with fish, Jesus told the disciples to bring some of their catch to shore—where He already had breakfast cooking. Jesus then looked at Peter and asked a very direct question: "Do you truly love me more than these?" (John 21:15).

"Yes," Peter responded. But Jesus wasn't done. Twice more He asked Peter about his love. The threefold question was fitting; just days earlier, Peter had three times denied that he even knew Jesus. Jesus was now giving Peter a chance to put all that behind him. John 21 is a beautiful story about forgiveness—about a new start.

Intellectually I knew this. But as I sat reading in my office, I was affected by this story in another away. The deep professional emptiness I'd been feeling found strange comfort in the image of the bursting nets. I longed for that kind of fullness in my own work. As the nets had surfaced, I felt a new clarity surfacing as well.

In the margin of my Bible, I wrote the words "11/00 I'm fishing." It was November 2000. My life was about to change.

## *Chapter 2*

# Born for This

We're supposed to follow our dreams.

That's what I'd grown up believing. Each of us has a work that we're literally born for. From the moment we're created, God places within us a natural desire for this work, and this desire only has to be awakened. For some, the desire might be making music, fixing things, caring for people—whatever gets your heart stirring. One of the most beautiful moments in our lives is when the desire already present within us is suddenly awakened. Our palms get sweaty, our stomachs get weak, and our hearts get stirring again. I had seen this happen many times with my students, and it seemed to be happening anew with me. The desire that washed over me on this morning was the desire to publish. I wanted to create a publication that would pull in a mass of folks the way Peter's net pulled in a mass of fish.

Until this moment, I hadn't realized how much I missed publication work and the deep satisfaction it brought me. I *loved* how I felt when I was putting together a publication. It was as though I'd entered another world—a world of words and images that needed to be brought together in just the right way. I wasn't good at many things, but I was good at this. It was completely me.

One thing I'd never attempted, however, was to start my own magazine, and the sudden idea of doing so appealed very deeply to me. I knew exactly the kind of magazine I wanted to create. It wouldn't be about celebrities, like so many other magazines out there. Instead, it would be about ordinary people.

A publication like this was deep in my soul.

*****

I grew up near Lake Wobegon—in the small Minnesota town of Detroit Lakes (population 7,106). On Saturday nights, my parents would tune our van radio to Garrison Keillor's popular variety show, *A Prairie Home Companion*. Often we'd be driving to Fargo with the Burgesons for an exciting evening of Chi-Chi's and a movie. Our town didn't have restaurants like Chi-Chi's, and our movie theater only had one movie at a time, for two months at a time.

Garrison Keillor's gift was storytelling, a segment he began each time with, "It's been a quiet week in Lake Wobegon . . ." As the studio audience clapped, we, the radio audience, shushed each other. *Shhh.* Keillor's monologue was a real treat for all of us; it was when imaginations came alive, when calm made a guest appearance. Keillor's voice was as soothing as the Vick's VapoRub he talked about, and he took his sweet time telling his tales—savoring the human comedy as much as we did. He told us about Johnny Tollefson, a gangly adolescent desperate to get out from under his parents' rules; about Harold Star, publisher of the *Herald Star* newspaper; about the Sidetrack Tap, where the regulars warmly welcomed the newcomers. "That's the news from Lake Wobegon," we'd say along with Keillor, grinning at each other, "where all the women are strong, all the men are good looking, and all the children are above average."

Most of Garrison Keillor's characters weren't real, but they reminded me of the very real characters in my own life—particularly the people I'd see at our small Adventist church each Sabbath, sitting in their usual spots. My family sat on the left side of the sanctuary, about halfway back. The Burgesons sat just behind us; the McTaggarts in the middle of the right section; the Nelsons and Umbers just ahead of them; and the Kleins well up front in the third row. Everyone knew to stay out of another family's row at church. The service itself seemed to flow better with all of us in our regular places.

Occasionally, however, we had a problem—visitors. One week during the prelude, I watched a visiting family stride down the main aisle and sit smack dab in the third row on the right—the Kleins' row! I couldn't believe my eyes. The Kleins had sat in that row every week for years. That was *their* spot, and someone else had taken it. *What will happen?* I wondered. A few minutes later, I watched the Kleins themselves enter the sanctuary, walk briskly down front, pause, conference together for a moment, reverse direction, and sink slowly and bewilderedly into the fifth row. I felt sorry for the Kleins. All those years, all that time invested in their row, and some hotshot family of five, probably from Fargo, had rudely bumped them two rows back. I waited for one of the church elders to leap off the platform, scold the visiting family, and order them to switch seats with the Kleins; but no one did a thing, and I felt just sick for my friends.

Church wasn't the only place that felt like Lake Wobegon. Often our home did too. One evening we were sitting by the fireplace when our cat strolled in. Mom suddenly got the giggles. She asked my little sister, Angel, and me if we wanted to hear a funny story about Dad and the cat.

Yes! we said.

Oh, Michelle, Dad said.

Mom told us how, the night before, the phone rang very, very late. Because the phone was right beside Dad, she just waited for him to get it. Mom said she could hear Dad saying, Hello? Hello? but for some reason, the phone kept ringing.

Hello, Nashes, Dad said, as the phone continued to ring.

Finally, Mom turned over to discover that half-asleep Dad had grabbed the cat rather than the phone.

Hello? Hello? Dad kept saying into the dumbfounded cat. Angel and I laughed our heads off.

*****

These were the stories I'd always enjoyed most—the stories of real life, told by regular people like us. And it seemed to me that a publication full of people's best stories would be every bit as good as a publication full of celebrity news and gossip. This idea—a magazine about ordinary people—welled up in me so deeply on this morning in November that I felt like there was nothing that would keep me from seeing it through. Nothing. This was what I had been created to do. It was deep in my soul. And I couldn't wait to talk to Dad about it.

## Chapter 3

# Dad and Me

*The best feeling of all was running through the yard looking back over my shoulder seeing my football spiraling off his hand toward me.*

As a kid, I'd felt close to my entire family—but in a special way, to Dad, since we were the only guys. On Sunday afternoons in the fall and early winter, Dad and I watched Minnesota Vikings football games together. We didn't watch football on Saturday because that was the Sabbath, but we more than made up for it on Sunday. The games started at noon, which gave us time in the morning to accomplish something worthwhile, as Dad put it, such as plowing snow for old people. I'd ride along with Dad in our brown Jeep CJ-7, eating beef jerky, listening to the Vikings' pregame show, and after we would plow a few driveways, we'd come back home, kick off our moonboots, and watch the game together. At halftime Dad threw me passes in the backyard. When it got too cold to throw passes outside, I'd run behind the family room sofa and Dad would lead me and I'd dive over the back of the sofa for an amazing touchdown grab.

Our all-time favorite game ever was when the Vikings were trailing the Browns 23–22, with only five seconds left on the clock. From forty-six yards away, our quarterback, Tommy Kramer, dropped back to pass and heaved a bomb to the goal line. A mass of Vikings and Browns converged in a frenzy. A Browns' defender tipped the ball back into the air—and then out of nowhere, Vikings' receiver Ahmad Rashad stuck out his arm, pulled the ball into his chest, and fell into the end zone for a touchdown.[1]

He—he caught it! yelled Dad.

He did it! I yelled.

Dad and I leaped and high-fived around the living room. We did it! We did it!

* * * * *

One fall Dad took us all to Minneapolis to see a Vikings game at Metropolitan Stadium. On the day before the game, Dad and I were playing catch just outside our hotel with my purple-and-gold Nerf football. Since we were staying across the street from the Met, Dad suggested that we walk over to the stadium parking lot and play catch there instead. *Wow,* I thought. *Can we actually do that?*

It was great playing catch in the parking lot of the Met—as though the stadium itself was looking down on us. Dad told me patterns to run, and I ran them with gusto: down and out, down and in, buttonhook, post pattern. My favorite was the fly pattern; Dad heaved the Nerf deep, and I sprinted under it, just like Ahmad Rashad. As we threw the football back and forth in the parking lot, we found ourselves getting closer and closer to the stadium itself. Dad noticed that one of the gates seemed to be swung open. We walked closer. Sure enough. The gate was wide open, and we had a clear view all the way to the green grass itself. The linesmen were chalking the field for tomorrow's game. How cool!

We can't go in there, can we? I asked Dad.

Well, let's check it out, he said.

Reverently, we walked inside the gate, down the tunnel, closer, closer to the field. Oh, the grass looked so green. No one seemed to pay much attention to us. Before I realized it, we had reached the end of the asphalt. Another step and we'd be on the playing field.

One of the linesmen peered over at us. *Is he going to make us leave?* Dad tilted his head sideways at me. The linesman paused, then nodded his approval. He understood the moment.

How about we throw a few passes? Dad said.

You mean on the field? I said. I couldn't believe what was happening.

Let's go for it, Dad said.

I took off full speed onto the field, my football soaring through the air above me. I pulled it in at the twenty-five yard line, dodged a field worker, then pranced into the end zone. I jogged back to Dad, whose grin was as big as mine.

We threw passes for about twenty minutes at the Met, forty-eight thousand red seats our witnesses. Then we jogged back through the tunnel. *Wait till I get to school on Monday.*

* * * * *

Twenty years later, when I got my big idea for a magazine, Dad was the first person I told.

After Cindy and I had decided to move to Lincoln, we invited Dad and Mom to move there too. Dad had never cared much for Orlando, and Mom was terrific with our girls—a modern-day Maria von Trapp. We thought it would be fun to live close together.

Though Dad had never worked in publishing, he had a good eye for new ideas. I drove over and told Dad about my idea for a publication that celebrated ordinary people rather than celebrities. Dad lit up. He loved the idea.

I said that I wasn't sure how I would distribute it. Maybe we could sell in some classified ads and drop it around town as we'd seen other community publications do. Would Dad be interested in helping me?

Dad nodded. Yes, he might be interested. He said that if we could launch the product in Lincoln, we could later look to franchise around the country. I suggested the name *The Front Porch*. Dad loved that too. It had just the right flavor.

Dad and I met most every evening, after our regular jobs, to talk about our plans. Mom and Cindy just laughed and shook their heads. They'd seen the look in our eyes.

One evening our discussion turned to how we might set up our business operation.

Well, Dad began, I guess every father dreams of being able to go into business with his son.

The statement surprised me. Dad was typically low-key. It wasn't like him to say something like this, but I enjoyed hearing it.

Dad explained, with the aid of a notepad, how he saw the structure of our company working. He said that since he would be providing the necessary computer equipment, software, and capital for our venture, he would own 60 percent of the company. I would own 30 percent. The remaining 10 percent would belong to the company in case we needed to bring in someone else.

I felt blood rushing to my face. Just 30 percent? Was Dad just kidding? Was he testing me? Why wouldn't we at least split it fifty-fifty?

I'm not sure I understand, I said. Why would I get only 30 percent?

Well, he said, because I'd be fronting the equipment and capital.

*Well, that's convenient,* I thought. I hadn't even been given the option of fronting capital. Apparently, Dad just assumed that I didn't have any capital to front.

I felt hurt by Dad, and I found myself looking for a way to hurt him back. I spoke slowly.

I feel like I need to ask you something, I said. Do you think you're more careful now with money than when you were with the business?

Dad looked up from his notepad.

* * * * *

It had been a decade since the crash. Dad had made a lot of money in real estate in the '70s and '80s. Dad played real estate as aggressively as he played Monopoly: buy, buy, buy, mortgage if you have to, go for broke. It got us ninety-five acres and a huge house at the edge of town—and a few years later, a beautiful cottage eight miles away on Lake Melissa as well. It also got Dad a migraine every Friday evening.

Dad didn't ever talk about the money he made, and I never considered myself a rich kid. But apparently, in the eyes of the kids at school, I was rich. Every winter we'd take a vacation to Florida, and when I'd come back tan, the other kids noticed. Poor little rich boy, some of them chanted in the cafeteria line. I didn't enjoy this at all.

In the spring of 1986, when I was fifteen, Dad and Mom sat us down. We were moving to Orlando for the school year. Dad and Grandpa were starting a new business—something about assisted living communities—and Dad needed to spend a year down there working on it. Then we would come back to Minnesota.

We moved to Florida in August. It was hot, but I liked the change of scenery, and I liked not being known as a rich kid. We lived in an apartment complex called the Verandahs. Dad and I played tennis almost every evening, then we took a cool dip in the pool. A few months into our Florida adventure, Dad's business seemed to get more and more involved, so we decided to keep coming back to Florida each school year. We'd spend the winter in Florida when the weather was cool—we found a nice rental home on a golf course. Then we'd beat the heat and enjoy the summer at our lake cottage in Minnesota.

No one enjoyed the lake more than Dad, who seemed to be happiest when he was whipping our inner tubes back and forth behind the boat. He'd come home from work by five, slip into his swim trunks and old blue terrycloth boating jacket, and take us skiing and tubing deep into the evening. With each passing summer, however, Dad seemed to be at the lake with us less and less—and in Florida more and more. It's the business, Mom said, looking increasingly worried.

By the fourth summer, Dad was flying to Florida every Monday morning and returning every Friday evening. He came back exhausted and angry. He'd storm into the cottage, change into his swimming trunks, and lower the boat into the water. Grab your ski, he'd say robotically.

The business was failing. Dad was getting a lot of phone calls in the evenings. Mom was crying. It was over.

Our final weekend in Minnesota, I stood in the lobby after church, waiting for Dad to finish playing the organ. The organ was silent, but Dad hadn't come out yet. I pushed open the sanctuary door and saw Dad sitting in the front row. His face hung in his hands; his shoulders shook. I didn't know how to feel. Dad was forty-three. I had never seen him cry before. I walked to the front and stood beside him.

Are you OK, Dad? I said.

I'm fine, he said, quickly wiping his face. All set to go, pal?

The next day we auctioned off everything we owned. The day after that, we drove in to Amoco, filled the tank, checked the hitch one last time, and headed down Interstate 94. We moved into a two-bedroom apartment in Orlando. It had a pool and tennis court, too, but Dad wasn't in the mood for tennis anymore. He just sat on the sofa all day, petting the cat.

* * * * *

*Hmm?* Dad said, a puzzled look in his eye.

Do you think, I repeated, that you're more careful with money now than when you were with the business?

He paused, seemingly taken aback by the question. Oh, I think so, he said quietly. When we were trying to save the business I probably took some more risks than I should have. But I think I'm more conservative now than I was then.

I immediately felt terrible for asking the question.

In the days that followed, I came to accept Dad's rationale that if he were fronting the capital, then he should have the higher stake in the company. But as we continued laying the groundwork, I got frustrated by other things. Often in our planning sessions, Dad would sit staring at our spreadsheets for long, long periods while I waited for him to speak. I felt useless sitting there while Dad worked out some unknown detail in his head, the minutes silently passing.

Dad? I'd say. Dad?

*Hmm?* he'd reply. Oh, I'm sorry, pal. I was just thinking.

---

1. http://www.youtube.com/watch?v=22O8IowjQSg.

# Chapter 4
# Going It Alone

Sometimes, even when you love each other, it's just better not to work together. That's the decision Dad and I came to, reluctantly but mutually. During one phone conversation, he paused and then said, I'd still like to do this project with you, Andy, but I'm not sure it's worth risking the strain.

Yeah, I know, I said.

I had seen this same dynamic with Dad and Grandpa. Through the years they had dipped in and out of a working relationship, and it seemed like when they weren't working together, they got along better. Sometimes the office isn't big enough for two family members. Dad and I put our business idea on a shelf and turned our focus to our weekly golf game together.

Privately, though, my dream of starting a magazine was alive and kicking. The core concept—celebrating ordinary people—was the same, but I needed the right way to distribute it. I needed a fresh idea.

In the spring of 2001, I was crawling my way through the bulky Sunday newspaper. As I attempted to find the sports section, a mass of advertising inserts fell into my lap: Wal-Mart, Kmart, Target, and Sears. I wondered how many people felt the way I did—overwhelmed by the sheer bulk of the Sunday newspaper. I also wondered how many people actually read the ad inserts compared to the newspaper itself.

I began to research this and discovered some intriguing data: the most popular sections of the newspaper (news, sports, comics) were read by 60 percent of readers. But the ad inserts were read by only 18 percent of readers. What was the difference? Interesting content. If these big retailers, I reasoned, would put some interesting content into their inserts, more people would read them. More people would see their ads.

I studied the inserts that came in the newspaper. I noticed one key difference in the Wal-Mart inserts. While the other companies used professional models, the models in the Wal-Mart inserts were the Wal-Mart employees themselves. *That's pretty cool,* I thought. Wal-Mart wasn't afraid to break from the airbrushed culture. I wondered about converting Wal-Mart's ad insert into a magazine-insert hybrid. *Wouldn't this make business sense?* I wondered. Wouldn't the content draw more attention to their products? A publication like this, it seemed to me, would not only be unique but would immediately become one of the largest magazines in the world. I even came up with the perfect name: *Wal-Paper.*

*****

As soon as the school year ended, I devoted myself to a summer of studying Wal-Mart. I wanted to learn everything I could about the business approach (pile it high and sell it cheap) and culture of the giant retailer, then present my publication idea.

Coincidentally, Cindy had graduated from a Christian high school, Ozark Adventist Academy, near Bentonville, Arkansas, where Wal-Mart was headquartered. And that summer just happened to be her ten-year reunion. I was even more excited about the reunion weekend than Cindy was. We would go a day early and scout out the area. Ahead of time, I pored over a map of northwest Arkansas, looking for interesting things. Yes, there was the White River where Sam Walton himself took the shareholders on float trips. How hilarious. And there was the new airport. I was delighted most of all to discover the massive Beaver Lake near Bentonville.

This lake looks huge, I said to Cindy.

Yeah, said Cindy. We used to go skiing on Beaver Lake. It's really beautiful.

Perfect! If I join Wal-Mart, we could even have a lake home within driving distance. I'd always wanted to have a lake home, just like Dad used to have. We'd have such a great time with the girls.

I booked a night at a lakeside resort for Cindy and me. I also contacted a realtor named Chad to inquire about lakefront property, explaining that we were looking at the possibility of moving to the area. Chad seemed excited by my call and offered to meet us lakeside in his boat and take us for a tour.

Oh, you don't have to do all that, I said.

It's not a problem at all, Chad replied. I'll get the boat gassed up.

Oh, brother, Cindy said when I told her about our pending boat ride with Chad.

Well, I told her, even if Wal-Mart doesn't work out, we might still be interested in moving to the area, right?

Well, I suppose! she said.

A true Southern boy, Chad was just the nicest guy. He met us at the marina and took us for a two-hour ride all around Beaver Lake in his boat, followed by three hours of home visits that he had specially arranged. *Hmm,* very nice, we said, nodding, as Chad pointed out the finer points of each lake home.

As the day dragged on, I felt increasingly guilty. Even by my own optimistic standard, I knew that I might possibly be wasting Chad's time, given that Wal-Mart didn't even know who I was at that point. After we finished our tour of lake homes, we said goodbye to Chad, with whom we'd grown very close, and headed over to Cindy's high school reunion.

*****

I had never attended any of Cindy's reunions, and very quickly I decided I didn't like them. Those doing the reuniting looked so happy and comfortable; Brandy, is that you? Oh, my word! It *is* you! For the rest of us, the spouses of the reunited, the weekend was filled with awkwardness. I finally got a reprieve at the afternoon meal, hosted by a wealthy local family, the Bakers. Cindy was visiting with Leslie Baker, whose eyes suddenly lit up when Cindy told her who she'd married. Leslie then told her husband, Phil, that Cindy Griffin had married the Andy whose writing they liked. Phil's eyes brightened, and he wandered over to my corner chair.

Are you free for a bit? asked Phil. I'd love to take you for a drive over to the office.

OK, sure, I said. I certainly wasn't doing anything else.

We hopped in Phil's BMW convertible and headed over to the offices of his publishing company.

Phil was fun. He told me cute stories about his work in publishing. When we got to the office building, Phil showed me all around. He seemed interested in making a good impression, and I felt flattered that someone regarded my presence so highly. We finished the tour in the warehouse. Phil stopped walking.

You know, Andy, he said, I wanted to bring you over here because we may be looking to expand our editorial operations in the coming months, and I've been following your writing for some time.

*Wow,* I thought. I sure hadn't expected it, but this was sounding a lot like a job offer. It certainly couldn't hurt in case Wal-Mart didn't work out for some reason. Phil might even be interested in my new publication idea. I savored the moment.

In fact, said Phil, some of the characters in your stories were especially enjoyable to read about, since you were writing about this area.

*Huh?* I felt a twinge of confusion. I had written stories, but they weren't about people in this area. I had written about Minnesota, not Arkansas.

I guess what I'm trying to say, Phil said, is that a few years ago I told myself that if Andy Demsky ever wanted to settle in this area, I'd love to hire him.

Phil smiled. I didn't. I stood there processing his word choice: *If Andy Demsky ever wanted to settle in this area, I'd love to hire him.*

*Who is Andy Demsky?*

After an extended pause, I found my voice. Hey, I said, thanks so much for what you said. Just to clarify something quickly. My name, you know, actually isn't Andy Demsky. It's Andy Nash.

We both stood there quietly. I could almost hear the gears turning in Phil's head. This had become a very awkward situation for him, too, considering that he had just offered me a job and everything. Finally, Phil just said, Oh, and began walking out of the warehouse to his convertible. I followed.

Phil and I still talked on the way back from the office building, but the dialogue didn't have the same festive air that it had on the way there. As we pulled into the driveway, I caught sight of Cindy. The look in her eyes asked, Why were you gone such a long time? And what were you and Phil talking about?

Oh, my word! she said as we drove off. He thought you were Andy Demsky the whole time? Oh, my word!

Who's Andy Demsky? I asked her.

Oh, he's a guy from this area who wrote some novels.

Well, I said, I guess I could have *pretended* to be Andy Demsky and just told Phil a few years down the line.

Cindy threw her head back, laughing.

* * * * *

I returned to Lincoln with my hopes still high. I mailed my proposal to Wal-Mart and waited to hear back. Finally, I did, in the form of a brief e-mail. A guy from the marketing department said that he had reviewed my proposal and found it interesting—but he said that Wal-Mart was content with their current product. Thank you for contacting us.

I sat staring at the message, a single driving thought in my mind. *No, no, no, no, no.* My whole summer of research couldn't just end with one short message. In the days that followed, I kept refreshing my e-mail in the hopes that Wal-Mart would catch the vision, but I never heard anything from them again. I did, however, receive several e-mail messages from Chad, who was just checking in to see how things were coming along.

## *Chapter 5*

# "The Front Porch"

It was a helpless feeling to have hit the wall (Wal!)—to be so dependent on the whims of others. I'd rather work twice as hard and have control than work half as hard and not have control. If Wal-Mart didn't want my help with their publication, it might be better to just stick with my own. *Wal-Paper* was out. *The Front Porch* was back in.

I liked the idea of distributing a magazine via the newspaper. But to get *The Front Porch* inside the hundreds of newspapers around the country—what a daunting task! There had to be an easier way. I began to think about *USA Today*.

* * * * *

In early September 2001, I went to lunch again with Chris Blake. Over Mexican food I told him what had been going on with me—how for the past ten months, around the edges of teaching, I'd been trying to find the right outlet for my publication idea. Each time I hit a wall, I said, I've just aimed for something better.

Chris smiled. Something better, he said. That's the way God works. He always gives us something better.

*USA Today* is interested, I said, but they want to see a prototype first. I just think people might be ready for a magazine like this.

A few mornings later, Chris and I were sitting in a staff meeting at college. Suddenly, Janya, the office manager, burst in. A second plane had hit the twin towers; another had hit the Pentagon.

*****

In early October, Chris and I took a vanload of our communication students to Chicago for a conference. The cloud of September 11 hung over us; we sang "God Bless America" at the end of every meeting. For one of the afternoon tours, we visited a large ad agency, where a brisk-talking executive told us about the latest trends. Someone asked her what advertisers are looking for.

I think what advertisers are looking for now, she said, after September 11, is a focus on hearth-and-home products. They're looking for something that's real.

Chris looked over at me and nodded.

*****

How would we pay for that? Cindy asked two weeks later. We were discussing the cost of a *Front Porch* prototype.

What we'd do, I explained, is take out a home-equity loan for twenty thousand dollars. It would more than cover the cost of the prototype. I'd go out to *USA Today* and present it after the semester ended.

Cindy sighed. Twenty thousand dollars was all the equity we had. It was everything we had.

Honey, I said, if you don't want us to do this, we won't.

It isn't that I don't want you to do it, Cindy said. I know how excited you are about it, and I completely trust you. I'm just not used to these types of decisions.

Born in Brazil, Cindy was the daughter of an American missionary family. With three older siblings and two parents on one income, she was accustomed to simple living. Her family had eventually returned to the United States, where her dad pastored several churches and taught his children the importance of frugality. Cindy said they almost never went out to eat.

*****

The prototype looked beautiful. The high-end magazine designers I'd hired, Dever Designs, finished it in mid-December, just in time for me to fly out to Washington, D.C., and meet with *USA Today.*

I didn't fly alone. When I made the commitment to *The Front Porch,* I knew that I was going to need help on the business end. Chris recommended that I talk with one of our colleagues, Mark Smith, who taught in the business department. Mark was both an attorney and a CPA; he was also six feet eight. Like me, Mark had grown weary of college teaching, but neither did he want to return to private practice full time. He wanted to avoid hourly based work altogether. His goal was wealth through leverage: build a business and watch it grow.

Over Indian food we discussed Mark's possible involvement in *The Front Porch.* I explained that I didn't have the money to pay staff right now, but if Mark wanted to invest his time, he'd get a chunk of the company. On a napkin I drew a pie with five slices. I would count his time the same as my time from that point forward: one slice of pie each. My ideas and time to that point would also count as one slice. The remaining two slices would also go to me since I was the one fronting the capital. The words had a familiar ring to them.

Mark studied the napkin and said he thought it looked fair. We had a deal. The company would be 80 percent mine, 20 percent his.

* * * * *

In most respects, the meeting with the *USA Today* executives went well. They complimented us on the prototype and seemed to feel comfortable with the match. They weren't going to stuff just any magazine inside *USA Today.* The only problem, they said, was that many of the prospective advertisers on our list were also clients of *USA Today.* These would be off limits to us.

*Well, that would have been nice to know earlier,* I sat there thinking. Without the ability to sell ad space freely, this was going to be very challenging.

One thing you could do, they suggested later that week, would be to acquire a sole sponsorship with a company that wasn't on their list, such as Wal-Mart.

Inside I laughed. *If they only knew.*

Mark and I talked. What should we do—try to operate within *USA Today's* advertising restrictions or throw off the chains altogether and try to get *The Front Porch* into local newspapers one at a time?

Because the Sunday paper in most cities already carried either *Parade* or *USA Weekend* magazine, we wondered about pitching *The Front Porch* to local newspapers as a boost to their weekday edition—say, the first Thursday of each month? Wouldn't that be appealing to them? And what about national advertisers? Wouldn't they be just as happy to have their ads appear in a Thursday magazine such as *The Front Porch* as in a Sunday magazine such as *Parade*?

I wondered how the weekday newspaper demographic compared with the Sunday newspaper demographic. To my delight, I found a fascinating piece of data: weekday newspaper readership was more slightly affluent than the larger Sunday newspaper readership.

This data was gold. We could position *The Front Porch* as value added to the weekday newspaper and as a more affluent demographic for the advertising community.

We'd found the formula. All we needed to do was sell it!

## *Chapter 6*

# 100 Newspapers

I was manic.

In early January 2002, Mark and I had pulled the trigger. We were going after local newspapers around the country. By late January, we had a promotional brochure ready to mail. Chris helped us create the brochure, and as he did, he began to get a twinkle in his eye. Prior to teaching, Chris had been a magazine editor and author. He was one of the best writers and thinkers I knew.

Chris, I said, are you interested in being part of this?

Let's talk, he said.

By the next day, Chris was *The Front Porch*'s vice president of editorial, joining Mark as vice president of business operations, and me as publisher. Chris dubbed us a strong three-legged stool.

*****

When the brochures arrived, together with our wives, we scheduled a Saturday night stuffing party at Chris's place. Chris cranked up the music, and we stuffed and laughed deep into the night. It didn't get much more exciting than this.

There were more than 1,400 daily newspapers in the United States, and we were set for an all-out blitz. *Parade* and *USA Weekend* were carried in 550 and 300 newspapers, respectively. They had been around a long time. If we could get in a good handful of newspapers to start, we could grow from there.

On Monday we mailed the brochures, flipped on a Web site, and waited. The first call came Wednesday from nearby Grand Island, Nebraska. The publisher said he was interested in the product but wanted exclusivity over the Lincoln and Omaha newspapers. We said No. He ordered anyway. The next two days brought a few more calls and Web orders. Not bad for the first week.

The second week overwhelmed us. Calls poured in from all over the country: Utah, South Carolina, Florida. We could tell where the mail was being delivered. Yes, said publishers and editors, we'd like to order *The Front Porch*. In the wake of September 11, the focus on ordinary Americans really appealed to them.

We struggled to keep up with the inquiries—Chris, Mark, and I were all full-time college professors. We put a system in place, dividing up call duty according to who wasn't in class at the time. Once Chris was on duty while the three of us were eating lunch at DaVinci's, a local Italian eatery. DaVinci's played festive Italian music in the dining area, so when the cell phone rang, Chris left our table and ducked into the men's restroom for some quiet.

Just as Chris said, Hello, this is Chris Blake, he heard someone say, I like my steak! *Mi piace la mia bistecca!* Italian lessons were blaring through the restroom speakers.

Yes, someone said, I'm calling about your new product, *The Front Porch* magazine.

Spinach. *Spinacio.*

Oh, yes, how can I help you?

Green beans. *Fagioli verdi.*

Well, we were wondering whether we could see the entire first issue.

Leg of lamb. *La gamba di agnello.*

We'll have the first issue ready to review in May.

Rare. *Raro.*

When Chris returned to our table, he was sweating profusely, his shirt soaked through. Well, that was fun, he said.

Another time I was on call while at home with the two girls. Just as the phone rang, Ally began to fuss. I rushed to our bedroom, out of earshot, to take a call from the *Augusta Chronicle*. The president was on his speakerphone with several other executives. This was a big deal.

Hi, this is Andy Nash. How may I help you?

The president proceeded to ask several questions about *The Front Porch*. As I answered, I could hear Ally coming down the hallway, trying to find me. She opened my bedroom door. I slid down between the bed and the wall.

Where are you, Daddy?

When should *The Front Porch* be released each month?

It should be released the first Thursday of each month.

Daddy, where are you?

Do you allow any space for local ad sales?

No, we don't.

*Daddeee!*

I got the order and hung up just as Ally found me and squealed. I wondered what the president of the *Augusta Chronicle* would think if he knew he'd just made a deal with a thirty-year-old dad cowering behind his bed.

Behind my office door at work I hung a map of the United States, and each time a new city ordered *The Front Porch*, we pushed in a pin. The *Tucson Citizen*, the *Washington Times*, the *Larned Tiller and Toiler*, the *Port Charlotte Sun*, the *Milwaukee Journal Sentinel*, the *Lincoln Journal-Star*—the pins kept coming. By the end of February, more than one hundred newspapers totaling a circulation of 3.1 million had signed up to carry *The Front Porch*.

We were overwhelmed. Not only had this figure exceeded our expectations, but as I discovered at eleven thirty Saturday night at my office, a circulation of 3.1 million would make *The Front Porch* the second-largest launch in United States magazine history.

The fish were leaping into the net!

# *Chapter 7*
# Fatherhood

From the moment our daughters were born, Cindy and I loved them to the depths.

The first time I kissed Ally's soft newborn forehead, I thought, *Oh, sweetheart, how can I be so in love with someone I just met?* As the early days turned into weeks and then months, Cindy and I savored her every stage: drooling, rolling, crawling, cruising, walking, and pedaling. The three of us lived in a small apartment outside Washington, D.C., and our most special times together were also our most simple: pushing Ally on the swings, taking walks on nature trails, meeting friends for ice cream.

I loved Ally with all my heart. And when Morgan broke onto the scene, I loved her too. Loved them, loved them, loved them.

This type of love came naturally to me. I had seen it modeled by my parents, who had seen it modeled by theirs. Mom and Dad were always there for us: every school play, every concert, every game. Twenty years later, I could still remember my very first time at-bat in Little League.

*****

I stepped to the plate and gazed out at the pitcher. He was big—probably eight years old. Maybe nine. And he threw the ball hard. *Man, did he throw hard.*

Go, Andy! Get a hit!

I panned the crowd behind the backstop to find my number one fan,

Mom, leaning forward in her lawn chair.

You can do it! Woo-hoo!

Behind her stood Dad. He didn't say anything, but he smiled and raised his eyebrows twice, which meant he hoped I'd get a hit, but if I didn't, no big deal. I tried my best not to smile at them because that wouldn't be cool. But I did. I couldn't help it. I was glad they were there.

Turning to the pitcher, I raised my bat like Rod Carew. The pitcher leaned forward for an imaginary sign, then reared back, his face contorted. The ball spun off his hand and shot toward me. I reeled to the right to protect my face, leaving my back exposed.

*Whomp!* Confusion. Pain between my shoulder blades. Tears in my eyes. Had I done something wrong? Was I out? I turned to the blurs behind the backstop. One of them had her hands over her mouth. The other clapped twice. Shake it off, pal, he said. Get on down to first.

I did. I got on down to first. As fast I could run.

* * * * *

I knew how lucky I was to have parents who were always there for me because, over the years, I'd known others who weren't as lucky. Once, after church, I was talking with a middle-aged man about our childhoods, and I mentioned how my mom was able to be home with my sister and me. He said how his mom always had to work full time while he went to child care.

Then his eyes lit up. For two weeks every summer, he said, his mom used her vacation time and got to be home with him. She'd have a big breakfast waiting each morning, and they would spend the whole day together. The man's eyes filled with tears as he described how special this was to him.

I looked forward to those two weeks all year long, he said.

Seeing this middle-aged man's emotions made me feel all the more grateful for my upbringing. No, we Nash grown-ups didn't always get along perfectly with each other, but we sure knew how to give time and attention to our kids.

We also knew how to give them stuff. Dad and Grandpa, especially, always seemed to get their greatest joy in giving gifts to their kids. And they gave us good gifts too: dogs and cats and horses; foosball tables and playhouses and water skis; trips to Big Sky and the Black Hills and Disney World—things we enjoyed together. That was the great thing about Dad and Grandpa. They didn't just give us stuff; they gave us stuff that they enjoyed with us.

When Angel and I were old enough, Dad bought Honda three-wheelers not only for us but for Mom and himself as well. On Sabbath afternoons, we'd take long winter trail rides, Dad in the lead, rocking wildly back and forth to make a good path through the snow. When the lake froze, we'd ride out on the ice, spinning hilariously. Once when it had snowed hard, Dad took the Jeep out on the lake and plowed a large oval ice track, complete with three-foot-high snowbanks. We raced our three-wheelers around the track; and when we lost control, we just slid comically into a snowbank.

I deeply desired these special memories for my own kids. As a teacher, however, I was never ever going to be able to afford them. I didn't make enough money teaching, and I didn't want Cindy having to work more than one nursing shift a week, as she was already doing. We both wanted her to be home with the girls. I found some additional editing work in the evenings, and that helped—but not enough to be able to give the girls the kinds of things Dad had given Angel and me when we were kids. And I sure hadn't gotten any type of boost from Dad, since he lost all his money just when I hit college. Dad's dad had given him a *huge* boost. Grandma had told me. Ironically, after we all moved to Lincoln, Dad had started making good money again—meaning he was able to give neat presents to the girls while I struggled along. I was quietly frustrated.

* * * * *

But soon these days would be coming to an end. The new business would allow me to give to my own children the way I *wanted* to give to them. Hey, it wasn't as if money were my primary motivator here. I was following my passion. But if following my passion also happened to bring in a boatload of money, then all the better. According to Mark's latest financial projections, *boatload* might have been too humble a term.

I showed the projections to Cindy as we sat in the hot tub late one night in the basement of our house. The hot tub was our primary luxury. We were giddy about it when we had found this house two years earlier. In fact, we were giddy about the whole house: only twenty-two years old, nearly fifteen hundred finished square feet, three bedrooms with closets, an eat-in kitchen, a fenced-in backyard with beautiful perennials; our first house—and it had a hot tub!

Here's what Mark is projecting, I told Cindy as I held the papers above water level. At 3.1 million circulation, with eight pages of advertising, here's what Chris will make.

Cindy stared wide-eyed at the six-figure payout.

Here's what Mark will make.

Cindy blinked.

And here's what we will make.

Oh, my word, Cindy said—exactly the reaction I'd been hoping for. As majority owners of *The Front Porch,* we'd be making more than a million dollars a year.

I wasn't done.

At five million circulation, I said, here's what we're looking at.

At ten million circulation, here's what we're looking at.

The projections fluttered to the floor.

The neat thing about being on the verge of great wealth was that Cindy and I knew it wouldn't change us from the people we were. I personally would continue to buy my clothes off the clearance rack—buy winter clothes in the spring, buy summer clothes in the fall. That was my philosophy, and it wouldn't change. And I didn't need a fancy watch either, just something cheap and functional. I'd eat at regular restaurants and leave great tips. I didn't want to be rich for me, but for others. People would see that in me and say what a regular guy I was.

I knew that Cindy wouldn't be any prima donna either. If anything she seemed nervous about our pending wealth. She didn't want it to change the girls. Apparently, she shared this sentiment with a friend of hers—how she didn't want our pending wealth to change our girls—because over the next few weeks the friend kept bringing up the subject. She seemed to be hinting that the least we could do was share the wealth. Cindy felt like it was causing some strain in their friendship.

Shortly after the newspaper bonanza, the weather finally warmed, and Ally and I took a walk to the park. She was now four—such a special age. Back and forth, back and forth, I pushed her on the swings. *Such a sweetheart,* I thought. This park was OK, but what I really couldn't wait to do was take the girls out in the boat with me. Then we could *really* have fun together.

*Wow,* I thought as I pushed, *I can't believe how many newspapers have signed up in a month. That's amazing. We'll have a huge print run—the second largest launch in U.S. magazine history! We definitely made the right decision in going with Quebecor for printing. Memphis is such a nice central location to print and ship all over the country. Now all we need is to get some advertisers on board—*

Daddy! DADDY!

It was Ally. She was shouting. Suddenly, I realized that she'd been saying Daddy over and over.

*Hmm?* I said. Oh, I'm sorry, sweetheart. I was just thinking.

# *Chapter 8* Keep Rollin'

As Ally and I walked back from the park, I silently cursed myself for the way I had tuned her out. I didn't want to do that. Being an attentive dad was very, very important to me, and I wanted to be able to turn off work when I came home. But it wasn't easy right now. Almost overnight, this thing had exploded. *The Front Porch* was no longer just a concept that I could roll around in my mind at my leisure; it was now a reality that was affecting a *lot* of people.

With a starting circulation of 3.1 million (much bigger than *USA Today*), *The Front Porch* was set for a massive print run. All we needed to do now was finish the first issue and sell ads. Finishing the first issue was the fun part. Finally, I could get back to doing what I loved most. Under the *Front Porch* nameplate, we placed a simple four-word slogan: Where People Share Life. For our first cover, we purchased the usage of a classic Norman Rockwell painting, titled *Marbles Champion,* and announced a Search for the Next Norman Rockwell competition. We also created three more contests: an invent-a-sport contest, a bedhead photo contest, and a nationwide columnist search with a one-year contract totaling twelve thousand dollars as a reward.

The rest of the magazine we carved into "rooms" and invited our readers to fill the rooms with their stories and memories, wisdom and dreams. As our promotional materials told it:

> In *The Front Porch* you'll find a little of everything. Drop by The

Entryway and browse through the mail stack. Laugh your head off in The Family Room as people tell about their funniest moments. Lounge in The Living Room as you listen to a contemporary American tale. Slip into The Kitchen for a great new snack idea, then to The Dining Room to meet Melia—your source for hospitality hints. Reflect on life's deepest questions in The Study; read a *real* love story in The Bedroom. Don't forget to peek into The Guestroom—you never know who might be there. Climb to The Attic for the best of yesteryear. Then trot out to The Backyard for a little fun and some advice swapping over the fence. And much more. Only in *The Front Porch.*

To establish the tone we wanted in our first issue, Chris put forward a story called "My Father's Kiss" he had personally edited years before. The writer, Lonnie Collins Pratt, told of being hit by a car when she was a little girl. Her face had been so badly damaged that she barely recognized herself. Toward the end of the story, Lonnie gazed into a mirror for the first time:

> Nothing could have prepared me for what I saw. Instead of the familiar glowing complexion, I stared at an image resembling a giant scraped knee. My eyes and lips were crusted and swollen. Hardly a patch of skin, ear to ear, had escaped trauma.
>
> When my father arrived with a magazine and my homework tucked under his arm, he found me staring into the mirror. Slowly he pried my fingers from the mirror, saying with each finger he loosened, "It isn't important. This doesn't change anything that matters . . ." He tossed the mirror onto a chair, then sat on the edge of my bed.
>
> "I know what you think," he said.
>
> "You couldn't," I mumbled, staring out the window.
>
> "You're wrong, though," he continued. He put his hand on my arm. "The people who love you have seen you at your worst, you know."
>
> "Right, seen me with rollers or with cold cream—not with my face ripped off!"
>
> "Let's talk about me, then. I love you, not your outside. I've changed your diapers and watched your skin bloom with chicken pox. I've wiped your bloody noses and held your head while you threw up in the toilet.

"I've loved you when you weren't pretty." He hesitated and then continued. "Yesterday you were ugly—not because of your skin, but because you behaved ugly. But I'm here today, and I'll be here tomorrow."

I turned to my father, feeling that these were all words, the right words, spoken out of duty—polite lies.

"Look at me then, Daddy. Look at me and tell me you love me!" My tone of voice defied and accused him.

I will never forget what happened next. As he looked into my battered face, his eyes filled with tears. Slowly my father leaned toward me, and with his eyes open he gently kissed my scabbed, oozing lips.

It was the kiss that tucked me in every night of my young life, the kiss that warmed each morning. A kiss echoing eternity. A kiss that works on twisted cursing lips.

My only scar, many years later, is one tiny indentation just above my eyebrow. But my father's kiss and what it taught me about love remain with me.

I loved this story, and I loved *The Front Porch*. And when we shared an advance peek with our pending newspaper carriers, they loved it too. Not a single one canceled.

To fund the magazine everyone loved, we would sell advertising. To get a feel for what we were facing, I phoned an advertising executive named Marek in New York to get his advice. His words made me break into a cold sweat. Most major advertisers, he said, won't even *look* at a new title until it's years along. So what you've got to do, he said, is to try to accelerate the process. You've got to find creative ways to get the attention of the big accounts. As an illustration, Marek told me about a new business hotel in Australia that had just added a state-of-the-art fitness center. They wanted to get the attention of key business people throughout the country, so they mailed out thousands of high-end tennis shoes to prospective clients. The twist? The hotel mailed only the *left* shoe. To claim the right shoe, the business person had to stay a night at the hotel.

I loved the example of creative marketing. It reminded me of something Dad had done when he ran Heritage Realty back in Minnesota. He produced thousands of golf tees with the words *Heritage Realty* printed on them.

When he went golfing, he'd toss handfuls of tees on the tee boxes for golfers to use. He sold houses because of golf tees.

Chris, Mark, and I discussed how we could creatively attract advertisers to *The Front Porch*. We were preparing our media kits to mail to ad agencies around the country. What if we also mailed a gift that creatively matched the flavor of *The Front Porch*? Like apple pies or chocolate chip cookies. We shopped around and finally settled on pans of cinnamon rolls from a great bakery in town. Yes, cinnamon rolls would work well. The pans perfectly fit the Express Mail boxes provided by the United States Postal Service, leaving just enough room for our media kits to slide in on top. Plus, cinnamon rolls were often eaten on front porches, weren't they? Yes, of course. Front porches were the *perfect place* to eat cinnamon rolls. If they arrived the next day, they'd still be plenty fresh. The frosting would be dripping from the mouths of the delighted advertising executives as they rushed to book space in *The Front Porch*.

We ordered forty pans of cinnamon rolls and picked up forty Express Mail boxes from the post office. Wow, with overnight delivery, this was going to be an additional chunk of change Cindy and I poured into this—nearly one thousand dollars. Chris helped defray the expense by dropping off a personal check for one hundred fifty dollars. In the memo, he wrote, Keep rollin'.

* * * * *

To this point, Cindy hadn't been highly involved in our effort. But forty pans of cinnamon rolls in our small kitchen seemed to motivate her. We slid in the pans, then the media kits. We folded the box tabs and sealed them.

Are you sure, she asked, that the rolls aren't going to slide around?

No, I said, I think they're in there pretty good.

She grabbed a sealed box. Well, just to make sure, she said.

As Cindy violently shook the box, we both burst out laughing and fell against each other. It was a welcome respite from a hectic afternoon.

The pace picked up again that evening at the main Lincoln post office. Just before closing, Cindy and I toted our forty Express Mail packages through a long line of customers who were obviously eyeing us. When we reached the front, the clerk asked whether we were sending anything perishable. Yes, I said.

Over the next few days, I tracked the cinnamon rolls to see what time they had arrived. Of the forty packages, about ten of them missed the promised time—meaning that we got a refund on the mailing expense but also meaning that these ad agencies were getting cinnamon rolls that were drying out by the minute.

All the cinnamon rolls arrived within three days of mailing—except for one that inexplicably arrived eight days later. It was the one we'd sent to the in-house advertising agency for the United States Postal Service.

# *Chapter 9*
# The Millionaire and His Wife

We were hugely disappointed. Compared to the enormous response we'd gotten from newspapers, the response from advertisers was paltry. My cell phone wasn't shaking at all with exciting reports from the sales team we had hired. When I called our reps individually to ask how things were looking, they just said, It's going to take some time.

Ad agencies aren't, by nature, quick movers. Though they wanted the public to be early adopters of the products *they* were advertising, the advertisers themselves weren't early adopters of new media. Only after a magazine had established itself in the eyes of the wider public would most ad agencies have the nerve to include it in their media strategy—never mind how good the magazine was. That left the magazine with only one way to establish itself: a huge war chest of cash to ride out the process. What we needed was someone with deep pockets who believed in our product as much as we did.

Chris had an idea. He had a pastor friend out west named Jimmy, who once had told Chris about a friendship he'd built with a wealthy local couple named Joe and Karen. Jimmy told Chris that Joe and Karen were some of the nicest people he had ever met. You would never know they were rich—they lived in a fairly modest house. Jimmy told Chris that if he ever had a good cause that needed financial backing, Joe might be worth contacting.

We considered *The Front Porch* to be a good cause.

Chris called Jimmy. Then Jimmy called Joe. Then Jimmy called Chris with Joe's number. Then Chris called Joe.

Hey, I'm not a salesman, Chris began.

That's good, Joe replied, laughing. Because if you were, I'd probably tune you out.

Chris and Joe talked about *The Front Porch* and about contemporary culture. Chris explained that we were different from other magazines—we weren't panting after trends and celebrities. We were focused on everyday life and ordinary people, in the tradition of great American magazines such as *Poor Richard's Almanack,* the *Saturday Evening Post,* and *Reader's Digest.* Joe seemed to resonate and asked us to mail him some information. We used Fed-Ex.

A few days later, Joe phoned me to say he was impressed with our concept. He thought people would be drawn to a magazine like this. He, too, had grown weary of celebrity culture. He liked the idea of something positive and uplifting. Joe said that he'd be willing to fly to Lincoln to talk with us. If it was OK, he'd like to bring Karen and his young adult son, David, along with him.

Of course it's OK, I said.

I was struck by how kind, even humble, this wealthy man was. To learn more about Joe, I phoned Pastor Jimmy. Jimmy told me that he had once invited Joe to his church.

I don't need no organization, Joe said.

Yes, you do, Jimmy shot back. And you'd better get your butt in my church.

Joe laughed. He liked Jimmy's grit. Did a pastor really just say that?

* * * * *

The morning of the meeting we were all nervous wrecks. What should we wear? What should we say? I was battling a terrible cold that made it hard to speak. Mark said he heard that snorting water really helped with this. I went immediately to the restroom, filled my hands with water, and snorted it. I was a team player. If the company needed me to snort water, I'd snort water.

We drove out to the airport, where Cindy met us. After lunch together, Cindy would show Karen around town in our minivan, which Cindy had vacuumed thoroughly earlier that morning.

Where do you think she'd want to go? Cindy had asked me, nervous about what a millionaire's wife might want to do.

I don't know, I said. Just whatever.

Thanks, Cindy said.

Straining our necks toward the western sky, we caught sight of Joe's plane. This was unbelievable—a multimillionaire and his family flying in to see *us*?

Joe, Karen, and David exited the plane and met us in the waiting area. They were dressed nicely but not intimidatingly. They weren't wearing diamond-encrusted robes or anything. Joe just wore black pants and an open-collared black shirt. We walked toward them for a chorus of hi's.

We drove Joe, Karen, and David to a warmly lit Italian restaurant called Vincenzo's in the Haymarket District, one of Lincoln's nicest areas. Within minutes, around the table, we could see how pleasant these people were. What a relief! They weren't boastful or condescending; they were nothing like the stereotypical millionaire and his wife on *Gilligan's Island.* They were just people.

Over dinner David told about some volunteer teaching he'd been doing at a Phoenix elementary school. He described an activity he'd recently done with the kids. He asked them a simple question: What would you rather have—a million dollars or a penny doubled once each day for thirty days?

The kids went crazy deciding what to do, David said.

I was grateful that David didn't ask what I would do. I just wasn't sure. It was tempting to pick the penny, but what if that option only got you a few hundred dollars? Ah! I couldn't decide! I looked at Mark, who just smiled. He seemed to know.

David took us through the math. If you double a penny once per day, he said, you end up with more than five million dollars.

Ha-ha! This was fun. It was fun to be talking about large sums of money. May it only continue!

*****

When the check came, both Chris and I quickly raised our hand for it. We wanted to make sure that Joe knew that *we* were paying for the meal. He had flown here in his private jet. We would take care of the rest.

After the meal, we split into two groups. Cindy and Karen departed in the minivan, and the rest of us piled into Mark's Cadillac. At six feet eight inches, Mark needed a big car, and on this day Chris and I were thankful he was driving a Cadillac. It sent a good message. We weren't total paupers here. Chris offered the "shotgun" seat to Joe, but Joe graciously waved it off—Chris was taller and needed the legroom. Joe sat in back between David and me. At one point, my knee touched the knee of a multimillionaire.

We headed for our meeting at Chris's house on the other side of town. Ahead of time Chris had suggested to Mark that we take Sheridan Boulevard. Sheridan Boulevard was Lincoln's most scenic street. It had mature trees and beautiful homes owned by doctors. Chris thought Sheridan Boulevard would make a much better impression than just taking boring, old Highway 2.

But, apparently, Mark hadn't gotten the message because he drove right past Sheridan Boulevard and headed for Highway 2. From the back seat I saw Chris mumbling to Mark.

Don't you wanna take Sheridan? Chris said quickly.

What? Mark mouthed back.

Sheridan would be nicer, Chris said.

Mark kept swiveling his head toward Chris. He wasn't sure what to do. Should he turn around and go *back* to Sheridan?

*Just drive,* I was mentally screaming from the back. This deal didn't hinge on whether we took Sheridan Boulevard.

* * * * *

The conversation at Chris's house was at first light, even humorous. We stood on the back deck, looking across the sloping yard to an adjoining city park complete with basketball courts. Chris said that when they were house hunting and their teenage sons, Nathan and Geoffrey, caught sight of the basketball courts, they went berserk. *Shhh!* Chris and Yolanda had glared at their sons. This wasn't exactly helping their negotiating power. We all laughed.

Chris pointed at the basketball hoop about seventy-five yards away. For several years he had been trying, from his deck, to make a basket using an Aerobie—an orange flying ring. Once Chris had hit the basket pole, but that was about it. Each time he missed, he drew a pencil line on a sheet of paper taped under his deck. He had tried more than two hundred times.

After the chitchat, we moved into Chris's dining area for our meeting. Ahead of time we had set the table with red *Front Porch* folders stuffed with our business plan and other important documents. I started the meeting and then passed the baton to Mark and Chris. As we moved through our agenda, everything seemed to be going very, very well. Joe asked a few questions but mostly listened and nodded. David didn't nod as much, but he seemed to be with us.

Mark moved to the bottom line: according to our projections, at the share we were offering, Joe would double his investment in three years.

Joe spoke. He had studied the projections on the flight out and wasn't seeing quite enough reason to think that he would get that kind of return. There were too many variables.

The room went quiet. I felt a sense of panic. Well, what if we doubled it? I said.

The moment I said the words, I knew how stupid they were. The sideways looks from Mark and Chris confirmed it. My remark made us look impulsive and weak. *Stupid, stupid, stupid!*

Joe didn't respond to my comment directly. He seemed focused on the conflict he was feeling, between liking us personally and being uncertain about the venture. Publishing just isn't my area of expertise, he finally said. This is different from what I usually do.

Joe said that he was still willing to consider this—but he'd like for himself and David to take a closer look.

Sure, we said, quietly. That would be fine.

Suddenly David came alive, as though a switch had been flipped. Speaking quickly, he told us he was going to need the full contact information for our sales reps, for our printer, and for everyone else involved in any way with the company. Mark nodded and said that yes, he'd be happy to supply all that information. I felt grateful to have someone like Mark on the team. A CPA and a lawyer all in one. That was very impressive. He was a perfect vice president for business operations.

Someone rang the doorbell. It was Cindy and Karen, back from a day of shopping. Cindy smiled. Everything seemed to have gone well. Karen was even carrying a few small bags. She must have enjoyed shopping in Lincoln, Nebraska. *Good. Good.*

Chris emerged from around the corner. He had slipped away for a moment, but now he returned smiling. He was holding something—a little gift of his own. It was his newly published book, *Searching for a God to Love.* Chris pressed the book toward Joe and Karen. This is for you, he said.

I looked at Mark, who appeared a little nervous. He seemed to be thinking the same thing I was thinking. Chris's little gesture here wasn't part of our plan—wasn't part of our plan at all. It wasn't like we weren't proud of Chris's book. It was a great book—a really great book. Good job, Chris. But Chris hadn't heard about Joe's previous reaction to church. How did it go again? Oh, yes. Joe had said, I don't need no organization. Let's just hope he doesn't say the same thing right now.

Karen looked cautiously at the book. Oh, I think we must have this already, she said, pushing it back at Chris.

Chris raised his hands. I want you to have it, he said.

OK! I said. We'd better let you guys get back home.

We all shook hands, a chorus of byes.

*****

The next Sunday morning I met Chris and Mark at a restaurant called Village Inn. Today we were supposed to hear back from Joe. Mark had provided Joe and David with all the information they had requested—all the due diligence that David could ever want. All we could do now was wait.

I set my phone to the loudest possible ring and placed it on the table. This was no time for vibrate. As we waited for our pancakes, we talked about the various scenarios. What if Joe said Yes? *High five.* But what if he said No? What if he said Yes but for a lower amount?

We could start smaller, I said. We could pull back and make the money last longer.

Mark nodded. Yes, that might be an option to consider.

Suddenly, my phone rang. It was Joe. I slipped away to the parking lot.

Joe got right to the point. Andy, he said, I think I'm going to have to pull out of this deal. I really like all of you guys, but I'm just concerned about how much time and money it would take to get the business up on its feet. The large starting circulation is exciting, but it would involve a lot of money.

I felt an empty feeling in my stomach. Yeah, I said quietly, I've been thinking about that too. We were just saying that maybe we could start smaller.

Joe paused. He seemed to be thinking. Well, he said, I'm glad to hear you say that. I would feel much better about that.

He paused again. OK, he said, you'll probably still need to raise some more funds to hit your target, but here's what I'd be willing to do.

Joe provided the amount he felt comfortable investing—about half of our target figure.

It was my turn to pause. Had Joe just gone from No to Yes?

Thank you very much, Joe, I said. Would it be OK if I just run this by Mark and Chris?

Yes, of course, Joe said. Just call me later and let me know.

I walked back inside the Village Inn; Mark and Chris looked up from their pancakes.

## Chapter 10
# Risk

Sometimes Grandpa Nash gambled. Grandma Nash told me. After their divorce, she would call me in college and talk to me about Grandpa. She was hurting. On a cruise once, she awoke in the middle of the night—and Grandpa wasn't there. She waited a long time, but he didn't come back. So she thought she'd go find him. She walked all over the ship, looking for Grandpa. Finally, she came to the casino. There he was—slapping down bills like he'd been doing it all his life. She wondered if he had.

I didn't like hearing these stories. For one thing, I had my own life to worry about. For another thing, I didn't want to picture Grandpa like this. I loved Grandpa and had always enjoyed the time we spent together. When I was a boy, Grandma and Grandpa lived just sixty miles away in Wahpeton, North Dakota, and they'd drive over frequently to see us. On Christmas Eve, I was especially eager. I'd press my face against the cold bay window, hoping to catch a glimpse of their dark blue Lincoln pulling into our long gravel driveway. The window caulking had a mildly musty smell, but I didn't really mind because it reminded me of the last time I was at the window waiting for them. Sometimes I'd close my eyes tight for several seconds and then partially open one eye, squinting hopefully through the snowflakes toward the road. The porch light made the snowflakes glimmer like starbursts—my own secret kaleidoscope. The show went on for several minutes, and sometimes I'd forget why I was standing there in the first place. But I was brought back by the sight of the big blue Lincoln floating up the driveway between the snowbanks. Grandma and Grandpa stepped gingerly out of the car and smiled big as Angel and I came racing outside. They told us how happy they were to see us again—we were growing up so fast.

Later Grandpa and Grandma moved to Sarasota, Florida, and we'd fly down to see them every winter, our faces pressed against the airplane windows. We'd stay a whole week at one of Grandpa's beach condos; but for the first night or two, Mom and Dad were going to stay at the condo alone, OK?—so Angel and I stayed with Grandma and Grandpa. Their home was right on a golf course, and when I got old enough to golf, Grandpa woke me up before dawn and made fresh-squeezed orange juice. Grandma joined in with omelets and waffles, and the three of us enjoyed breakfast together. Angel slept in.

As Grandpa and I rode in the golf cart, he talked freely with me. He told me how, as a boy, he had once caddied for Babe Ruth. He told me that his favorite hymn was "The Savior Is Waiting." That song got to him every time, he said. I liked how openly Grandpa spoke. In this way at least, it seemed like I was more like Grandpa than Dad. Dad didn't speak openly about much of anything. He held it all in.

Your dad always held it all in, Grandpa said. It's just the way he is.

Grandpa told me how proud he was of me—that I was a good Christian young man and that he had high hopes for me. You're the only Nash boy left, he reminded me. You're the only one that can carry on the family name.

* * * * *

While I didn't like hearing about Grandpa's gambling, I wasn't terribly shocked. When the business failed and Grandpa and Grandma divorced after nearly fifty years, there were reasons—and gambling was only one of them. Once worth big money, Grandpa had risked everything they owned to try to save the business. He had mortgaged their Florida home and their North Carolina mountain cabin. He had signed Grandma's name without her knowing it. She told me about this too.

After the divorce, Grandpa stayed at a friend's place and took a job at Wendy's stocking the salad bar: the sixty-seven-year-old former tycoon now making sure there were enough croutons. But Grandpa really didn't seem to mind. Broken and humbled, he seemed almost relieved by the absence of the business pressure. At one point Grandpa wrote to Dave Thomas, the founder of Wendy's, thanking him for the work. Dave Thomas himself wrote him a nice letter back.

After the divorce, Grandpa and Grandma still spent time together. On Sunday afternoons Grandpa came by to mow the yard, and Grandma cooked supper for them. They lingered and talked, and as evening fell, she sent him off with casseroles and sandwich spreads for the week. Grandpa told me all about this in his own phone calls to me. He said that he hoped he and Grandma could reconcile.

But the wounds apparently ran too deep. After a few months Grandpa moved to the Northwest where he took a job hauling around photo equipment for Kodak stores. He remarried two years later; Grandma never did.

* * * * *

The other reason I wasn't shocked about Grandpa's gambling is that, deep in my soul, I understood the draw. From my youth I had felt the strange thrill of the uncertain outcome. This was partly why I liked watching sports so much because on any given Sunday you never knew who was going to win. Once in my *Viking Report* magazine, I saw an advertisement that claimed to know who was going to win each Sunday football game. This sounded interesting, so I filled in my home address and mailed off the reply card for my "free week of picks." For the next two decades, my parents received promotional mailings from Las Vegas bookies.

My favorite childhood board game was Risk—where each player started with a small territory and tried to conquer the world. To me, the best feeling in Risk wasn't when you had amassed a large empire and proceeded to wipe everyone else off the map. The best feeling was when you were the *underdog*—when you had only a small territory and, against all odds, you rolled the dice and took down the giant.

I never rolled the dice for real. Gambling was on the list of things Christians didn't do, along with drugs and drinking. My tender conscience prevented me from even getting close to it.

* * * * *

When I was nineteen, I decided to volunteer a year as a student missionary in southern Thailand, teaching conversational English and Bible seven hours a day. Over the holidays, I joined my coworkers Jeff and Roger on a trip to Hong Kong. On New Year's Day, we didn't have anything much to do, and I noticed an advertisement for horse racing at a nearby race park. It sounded interesting to see—just for the culture and everything.

As we sat waiting for the first race, I looked at the race card detailing the horses and their odds. Just for fun, I announced to the guys that I was pulling for a forty-seven to one long shot called Spellbound.

The race started, and I fixed my eyes on Spellbound. Coming out of the first turn, Spellbound was somewhere in the mix—not in front but not in back either. I was riveted.

Down the first straightaway, Spellbound began to gain ground. *Come on.*

The race announcer suddenly came alive. Spellbound makes a move on the outside! he screamed.

My heart pounded. This was awesome!

It's Spellbound on the final turn! Down the backstretch they came, Spellbound in the lead. I couldn't believe it. I elbowed Jeff. Did I know how to pick 'em or what?

Suddenly, as though downshifted, Spellbound began to slow and slow some more. The other horses charged past him, one after another after another. Spellbound slipped to the back of the pack. He seemed to be worn out.

Jeff laughed. Maybe there was a *reason* Spellbound was a forty-seven to one long shot.

I smiled meekly, the adrenaline dissipating from my system. *Wow,* I thought. I couldn't believe how emotionally invested I'd felt in this race.

It's a good thing I don't gamble, I told Jeff on the way out. Because if I ever started, I'd probably never stop.

* * * * *

It was funny. The way I felt when I saw Spellbound lurching out of the gate was a little like the way I felt when Mark, Chris, and I sat around the table at Village Inn and made the decision to start the business. The rush of adrenaline felt familiar.

There was an important difference between the two, of course. Unlike mere spectators at a horse race, we were *involved* in what was happening; our effort would help *determine* the outcome. We had some level of control here. Still, we were taking on some pretty big horses—and we didn't have a lot in reserve. Even though we'd decided to launch much smaller—at a circulation of 1.3 million rather than 3.1 million—there was still a large element of risk here, and we now had someone betting a lot of money on us.

It wasn't that I wanted us to be in this risky position. I wanted us to have a large war chest of cash. But in a strange way, the fact that we were going against the odds made the venture all the more exciting to me: like a forty-seven to one long shot taking on the heavily favored. If and when we did succeed with a relatively small amount of cash—and I fully expected us to—then this would make an even more amazing story (praise God) than if we had started with a large amount of cash.

It was early April, only two months after we'd begun our effort aimed at newspapers. Mark and I notified Union College that we were leaving. Chris would continue teaching but would work full time during the summer. The word began to spread; three college teachers were attempting to launch a large national magazine. The *Lincoln Journal-Star* did a story on us. With increasing frequency I was getting calls from friends who had heard about the venture. It felt as though they were gathering around me—sharing in my high-rolling experience. Particularly intrigued was an editor friend from Washington, Cliff Goldstein, who phoned several times a week as he drove home from his eight-to-five job.

When I had told Cliff the previous fall that I'd invested twenty thousand dollars of my own money to develop the prototype and promotional materials, Cliff was astounded.

You're using all of your home equity? he said.

When I now told him that I was leaving my teaching job to pursue this dream, he could barely get his head around it. You're a brave man, Andy, he said. I liked the attention I was receiving from Cliff and the other guys. I liked that they thought starting such a high-risk undertaking was such a hard decision. But, to me, the decision didn't feel *that* hard. Taking a risk like this almost felt natural.

For Cindy, however, none of this felt very natural at all.

# *Chapter 11*
# Faith

When it came to investing all our money—and quitting my job—there was only one person whose opinion really mattered to me: Cindy.

Cindy and I had always agreed on the important things—our view of God and the values we wanted to instill in the girls. But we brought very different temperaments and approaches to life. Cindy put a high value on not making a mistake; I put a high value on not missing an opportunity. Cindy was extremely cautious, even pessimistic at times. If we were taking a trip, Cindy would immediately begin listing all the things that could go wrong—starting with the flight itself—until she'd receive assurances from me. If Cindy was considering a new part-time nursing job or responsibility at church, she would always run down her own skills, waiting for the pep talk from me. I looked to Cindy in a different way. Since I was, by nature, much more optimistic, I depended on Cindy to slow me down—to talk me out of getting a Newfoundland puppy or moving to Turkey. Neither of these processes, my pep talks or Cindy's mashing on the brakes, had ever been very enjoyable for either of us; they sometimes came in the form of a spitting-mad argument. But they also usually ended with us in step again—and going out to eat, which we both enjoyed.

The dilemma we felt with *The Front Porch* was what approach to take. Was this the time to play it safe? Or was this the time to go for it—to let it all hang out and never have to wonder *What if?* As much as I favored the second option, I wasn't going to make the decision alone. Deep into many nights we talked. The only reason, Cindy said, that she was even open to this at all was that she believed in me. My ambition was what she liked so much about me in the first place.

The other factor was faith itself. As I explained to Cindy, I believed that that the Lord of all creation had inspired me with *this* creation. I believed that if I honored Him in all my dealings and in my personal life, His blessings would pour out. As Psalm 37:4 said, "Delight yourself in the LORD, / and he will give you the desires of your heart." Cindy nodded. Yes, she believed this too. But still, this was a huge decision.

One evening Cindy brought home a bag full of smooth river rocks and a pen with a gold marker. Because this was going to be a special period in our lives, she said, smiling, she thought I might like to memorialize each step along the way, the way the Israelites had memorialized their crossing into the Promised Land by bringing stones from the Jordan River along with them. Cindy's gesture meant a great deal to me. For the first time, she seemed fully on board. With the gold marker, I emblazoned each rock with the good things that had happened—Mark and Chris joining the effort, one hundred newspapers signing up, and now Cindy's support. Then I placed the rocks in a metal holder. It looked like a little altar. Each time something good happened, I placed another rock on the altar. The little altar sat on a table in our living room, a memorial of how we were in this together.

* * * * *

I knew that the most important thing that I could place on the altar of faith was my own life. As I'd studied in the book of Romans, we were to offer ourselves as "living sacrifices, holy and pleasing to God" (12:1). Though I was only thirty-one, I had seen plenty of immoral behavior over the years, both personally and professionally. Whatever else happened, it was very important to me that I conducted myself in an upright fashion. I believed that if I did, the Lord would honor it.

When we opened our offices in May, I began each day with the Lord. I'd sit at my desk reading *My Utmost for His Highest* and Scripture itself. Whatever I read, I prayerfully considered what it meant for my new business. In fact, it was hard to read anything *without* thinking about my new business. Even at church I thought about my new business. This bothered me a little—the fact that I couldn't get the business off my mind—but this was just the stage I was at right now. I needed to be focused. Things would level out later.

Sometimes I'd return to John 21, remembering how this passage had helped bring clarity to my life's work. It was my private reservoir of faith. As I read commentaries on this passage, I learned that the place where Jesus had filled the disciples' nets was now called Tabgha—an Arabic corruption of the Greek word *Hegtapegon* meaning "seven springs." Tabgha's fresh warm water on the northwestern shore of the Sea of Galilee was an ideal place for fishing. That's why Peter and his partners liked this spot so much. Tabgha was a fisherman's paradise.

Typically fishermen fished at night, when the fish were less likely to see the nets. When morning broke, the fishermen cast their nets on the dark, or shadowy, side of the boat, to give themselves a final chance at a few more fish. That's what was so interesting about Jesus' shoreline instruction to the disciples, to cast their nets on the other side of the boat—the "right side." This was the light, or transparent, side of the boat—the side of faith. By acting in faith, Peter and the disciples were rewarded with a huge catch.

# Chapter 12
# The Big Day

We launched *The Front Porch* on July 4, 2002.

That morning I woke up thinking about the 1.3 million copies of my magazine landing with a thud on the doorsteps of people's homes—and in a few lucky cases, their front porch itself. Our home was one of them, but Cindy and I weren't there. We had decided to attend her family reunion in Maryland. I knew I'd be really busy after the launch, so this would be our last chance for a break.

When I came downstairs for breakfast, I saw Cindy whispering excitedly to her older brothers. OK, Andy, she said, smiling. Shall we take a little drive to town?

I smiled back. We both knew *The Front Porch* would be carried inside the *Washington Times,* which was distributed in Maryland.

We drove to a nearby convenience store and walked inside—Cindy running the video camera.

Sure enough—there was a big stack of the *Washington Times*. I picked up the top copy and felt inside for the smooth-coated paper of *The Front Porch*.

Well, here it is, I said, grinning.

Cindy let out a scream and threw her arms around me. I felt so happy. This was the moment I'd worked so hard for.

*****

It was funny. One of my expectations about running my own business was the tremendous amount of freedom it would bring. Rather than being locked into someone else's schedule, I'd make my *own* schedule. I'd have complete control over the decision making and be able to come and go as I pleased.

*Goodbye, everyone. I'm taking my daughters out for ice cream this afternoon.*

*Goodbye, Andy! We'll take care of everything. Kiss those girls for us.*

Theoretically, I did have this freedom; in the two months since we had opened our office, I knew that I could leave whenever I liked. But in actuality this wasn't happening. I wasn't leaving work any earlier than I had at my previous jobs. In fact, I had to force myself to leave at 5:30. There was just so much to do, and well, what could I say? As the head honcho, I was often needed to do it.

That's why this moment at the convenience store was so enjoyable. After months of hard work, I finally got to hold the fruit of my labors in my hands.

That'll be fifty cents, the cashier said.

*****

We drove back to the house where the kids were outside launching bottle rockets. The girls yelled for me to come join them. I waved and said I'd be out in a minute—I just had to check something.

I went inside and logged on to *The Front Porch* e-mail account. I couldn't believe what I was seeing. Article submissions were pouring in from readers all over the country. Hundreds of them. Every time I hit refresh, the e-mail account spit out more submissions.

This was great! We had cast *The Front Porch* as the people's magazine, and the people were responding in a big, big way. They were sharing the stories of their lives.

We were getting letters too—tons of them. I settled into the chair.

> I just wanted to say thank you for starting *The Front Porch.* It is the most interesting and wonderful magazine that I have ever read. I hope this magazine will be an enormous hit.—L. A. Hutchens, Dobson, North Carolina.

*The Front Porch.* Vol. 1 No. 1 July 4—our nation's birthday. You embody the hope of every American in our secret heart. In our imperfections we have so many unrealized dreams. You've brought the warmth of Norman Rockwell, the cheerfulness of an underwater photographer in a bright pink bathing cap. At a time when so many Americans are hurting, stumbling in the dark, we surely need to celebrate kindness, goodness and decency in everyday life. *The Front Porch*'s premier issue has made a superb first impression.—Lois Bartlett, Centreville, Virginia.

It was so gratifying to read the endless flow of articles and letters. I couldn't believe that my idea had actually become reality—that people liked it so much. This publication was not only going to give me professional satisfaction again, but someday it was going to give my family the kind of life we dreamed about.

I logged off and went outside to launch bottle rockets with the kids.

When I returned to the office the next week, everyone else was just as excited about the public's reaction to *The Front Porch*. Together, we read the glowing letters coming in. Here are a few more.

The concept of your magazine, celebrating ordinary people, is brilliant. Congratulations and thanks for giving us the opportunity to share the many aspects of our lives with others.—Roxanne Rivers, Willimantic, Connecticut.

My wife Jennie just showed me your new publication and asked who sent it to us, saying that she and our 9-year-old daughter read it yesterday and really enjoyed it. She was impressed when I told her it was in the *Washington Times*. Both of these lovely ladies, my wife in particular, are uncanny bellwethers for the success of media products and enterprises, so it seems that your first effort is well produced and well targeted. Well done!—Doug Menefee, Alexandria, Virginia.

It's great. What took you so long?—Sue Brown, Sweetwater, Texas.

Our most meaningful feedback of all came from Joe, who called from

Phoenix to congratulate us on a great first issue. Joe's call meant a great deal to me. I wanted so much to succeed for him, and I thought we had just the people to do it.

Beyond Mark, Chris, and me, we had staffed our office with a small team of young people: a new college graduate, Jill, who worked full time; and on an hourly basis, several current students that I'd had in class—the cream of the cream. This was great. I still got to be with my students, but we got to build something together. This was way better than talking about commas and periods.

The student workers' primary task was to sort through the hundreds of submissions pouring in. At a rate of three thousand a month, we were getting a higher submission rate than even *Reader's Digest*—the king of reader response. We were also getting a heavy response to our contests: the invent-a-sport competition, the bedhead photo contest, and the national columnist search, which brought in more than six hundred entries alone.

Gradually, we worked our way to our columnist winner: a single mom and small-town newspaper editor named Debra LoGuercio. Her cover letter had cleverly opened with the words "Pick me! Pick me! Pick me!" We loved Debra's writing. She wrote about everything from the humor of adopting a bunny to the pain of visiting her dad in the nursing home.

Debra was perfect for *The Front Porch,* and when we called to tell her that she'd won the one-year contract, starting in January, she could barely speak. I was so happy for Debra. It was so much fun to bring joy to people's lives.

The positive reaction we were getting anecdotally was confirmed by an independent readership study we ordered in early September. When asked how they compared *The Front Porch* to *Parade* or *USA Weekend*, the two industry leaders, readers said they preferred *The Front Porch*. But not only that, they preferred *The Front Porch* by a margin of six to one.

Fish leaping out of the water! Fish turning cartwheels midair!

## Chapter 13
# Money

As much as people loved *The Front Porch,* we weren't ready to celebrate yet. Love didn't pay the bills.

Our ad sales were showing some positive signs. In mid-July, Laura from Bose called, asking if we had indeed printed. When we told her we had, she immediately booked two full-page ads. We were booking other advertisers, too, not the big-dollar clients yet but plenty of direct-response clients—vacuum cleaners, floor lamps—who were willing to try us out. These same clients also bought space in *Parade,* and we were told that they were getting a better response with us. By our September issue, we sold enough ads to be halfway to profitability. It looked as if we might just make it without having to raise more money. From everything we were hearing, this would be a phenomenal feat. Another newspaper-carried magazine had apparently raised twenty-seven million dollars in venture capital—and after three years, still wasn't profitable. Later, *Life* magazine would return as a newspaper insert, backed by fifteen million dollars—and even *Life* wouldn't make it. So for us to make it with only a small fraction of that amount would be a real success story—especially in the uncertain economic climate.

In the early part of 2002, it had seemed as though the economy might finally be rebounding from the 2000 dot-com bubble burst and the 2001 terrorist attacks. Investors were again dangling their feet in the water, hoping that the worst of it had finally passed.

On September 24, 2002, we learned that it hadn't. The Dow sank to its four-year low; the NASDAQ hit its six-year low. Weary of the roller coaster, investors and businesses began pulling in for a long winter. One sales veteran told us that the advertising outlook was the worst she'd ever seen. To ride this out, we were definitely going to need more money.

*****

*Should I call him again?* I wondered. I didn't want to, but we didn't have a lot of options here.

Months earlier, one of our student workers had told me about a guy in Florida that her father knew. Mr. Turk was a wealthy hotel owner in Cocoa Beach who had once played football for the Oakland Raiders. Periodically, back in the spring, I had called the husky-voiced Mr. Turk to see if he'd like to invest in *The Front Porch*. He had always acted somewhat interested; in fact, at one point he had told me that he was going to have his bank wire money to us. But no money had ever come, and I'd gotten fed up with the song and dance. The last thing I felt like doing was calling Mr. Turk again. I picked up the phone and dialed.

Mr. Turk, I'm glad I caught you.

Andy, my boy.

I just wanted to see how you're feeling about investing in *The Front Porch.*

What are you offering?

We could do twenty percent of the company for 1.7 million dollars.

I'll think about it. Call me back.

*Click.*

Same old story. Call him back. This was exactly how he'd acted before.

But I did call Mr. Turk back. I called him back many, many times. And every time I called, the conversation was the same.

Mr. Turk, this is Andy.

Andy! How you been?

Good. Would you like to invest?

Maybe. Call me back.

I *hated* talking to Mr. Turk. I hated that his stupid Cocoa Beach phone number was ingrained in my head. But I couldn't seem to stop calling him. Whenever he showed some interest in investing, I felt as if I was on an immediate sugar high. Maybe this was the call that would change our fortune.

*****

I'm eighteen and lying in the loft of our lake home in Minnesota. Dad is downstairs talking on the phone in a way I've never heard him talk before. His voice sounds plaintive, imploring.

Hi, this is Chuck Nash calling. May I speak to Mr. Abidea, please?

Dad waits on hold for a long, long time. Then he hangs up and calls again.

May I speak to Mr. Abidea, please?

All I know about Mr. Abidea is that he's in Panama and he seems to be Dad's last hope for the business. I've never heard Dad sound so desperate.

Mr. Abidea, please?

*****

Mr. Turk, if you're ready to move forward on this—

Call me back. *Click.*

I tried everything with Mr. Turk. I called him first thing in the morning. I called him late at night. I called him on the conference phone with Mark, Chris, and Jill sitting around the table. At one point, Jill seemed to develop a crush on Mr. Turk. She said he had a nice voice. Thanks, Jill. That's helpful.

Finally, I decided I needed to visit Mr. Turk in person. I flew to Orlando and drove over to Cocoa Beach.

My first thought as I entered Mr. Turk's office was that I needed to phone Jill and say, He may have a nice voice, but I'm not sure you'd like the rest of him.

A massively overweight and unkempt, older white man, Mr. Turk looked like Jabba the Hut. He sat behind a large wooden desk that featured, among other things, a can of spray deodorant and a bottle of mouthwash.

When I introduced myself, Mr. Turk stumbled to his feet and said, Here, I'll show you around.

We took a five-minute golf-cart ride around the resort grounds. Afterward Mr. Turk said he'd driven strictly from memory because he was now completely blind.

I rolled my eyes. That was impossible. There was no way he was completely blind.

We talked for a few minutes in his office as several other men walked in and out freely. Only one of them looked normal. Before I realized it, Mr. Turk himself had slipped away. Thirty minutes later, he still hadn't returned. I later found him upstairs at his sports bar. *Oh, brother,* I thought.

I left Cocoa Beach with neither a meaningful conversation or a check for 1.7 million dollars; but a few weeks later, a friend's wedding brought me back to Orlando. Against my better judgment, I drove over to Cocoa Beach to try again. As bizarre as my previous visit had been, the fact remained that Mr. Turk did appear to have some money—and we needed it.

This time Mr. Turk was even more elusive. Look, I said as we sat in his sports bar, if you don't feel this in your gut, then you shouldn't do it.

That's the problem, he said. I *do* feel it.

I wandered downstairs to Mr. Turk's office, where his normal-looking friend was dropping off some papers. Let's have lunch, he said.

Over Chinese food, the man explained that Mr. Turk had *once* had a lot of money, but he didn't anymore. He was deeply in debt. He was just an old man who was broke.

I sat there, stunned. Apparently, I had successfully convinced Mr. Turk to invest his money. The only problem was that he didn't have any money to invest.

I left my fortune cookie on the table, unopened.

# Chapter 14
# Fall

It was mid-November 2002, two years since I'd gotten the inspiration for this magazine. At that time it was just me. Now it was me and seemingly half the world. When I pulled into work, I didn't rush inside as I used to. I just sat in the parking lot for a while, gazing up into the large oak trees outside our office building. Most of the leaves had fallen from the trees, and I just stared up into them, studying how the trunk turned into limbs, how the limbs turned into branches.

At that moment, on interstates everywhere, dozens of semitrucks loaded with the December issue of *The Front Porch* were traveling from our Memphis printer to the shipping docks of newspapers all over the country. These newspapers had no idea that this issue would be their last. They weren't going to like that very much. Neither were our sales representatives. Neither were a lot of other folks about to be affected by our sudden and desperate change of course. These people were like the branches on this tree. Like it or not, they all shared a common root: me. I was responsible for all of this.

Please, Lord, I prayed. Please.

Everything had happened so quickly. After the Mr. Turk debacle, we thought our luck might be turning. Mark had been nurturing a promising dialogue with a kind older couple named Jake and Ella from here in town. A big teddy bear of a man, Jake *loved* the premise of *The Front Porch* and had approached us about investing. Jake and Ella didn't have the big money we needed, but they were willing to invest a smaller amount. Jake was so excited about his involvement with *The Front Porch* that even before we officially signed an agreement, he invited his family into our offices for a check-writing ceremony and celebration, complete with a smiling group photo.

But soon the smiles began to fade. The ad climate was getting worse and worse. In fact, with the sinking economy and the paltry new ad projections for our November and December issues, the additional investment from Jake and Ella wouldn't even fund us through the year's end.

I had an idea. What if we changed our business model? What if we played to our strength—our readers themselves—and switched to subscriptions? We could announce the change in our December issue, offering individual subscriptions for fifteen dollars a year. If enough subscriptions came in—ten thousand or so—we could still make it.

Jake asked how much we would need to get us through. We told him we'd need more than twice his original commitment. Jake said he'd put up the money if he could have an additional stock option in the future. When we shared the idea with the other investors, they were glad for the additional funding but cool toward the future stock option. We were running out of time. I decided that, if necessary, I would give up the additional stock myself. We had to get this done. We ordered the print run.

A few days later Jake walked slowly into the office. He'd been having second thoughts. He'd been talking with his family. He had decided not to invest in *The Front Porch* at all. He didn't think it had a strong enough foundation.

But we've already ordered the December issue, we told him. We're on the hook for that.

Jake didn't say anything, but his face turned very, very red.

*****

Over the years, whenever work had gotten stressful for me—though nothing had ever gotten *this* stressful—I knew that I could always find an oasis of support at home with Cindy. She had always given me the gift of thoughtful listening and genuine interest in my career. When I shared something about my day, Cindy was always right there with me. But lately something had been different about Cindy. Her deep blue eyes had a faraway look. Two weeks earlier she had come home from the health club looking frantic after an early morning spin-cycling class. In the middle of the workout, she said, her heart had suddenly started racing uncontrollably. She couldn't get it to slow down. She had requested an ambulance but then managed to drive home.

Cindy's doctor put her on a heart monitor and sent her back to the health club. When he saw the results, he told Cindy that she had supraventricular tachycardia (SVT)—sudden episodes of a rapid heartbeat. SVT, said the doctor, wasn't necessarily serious. It could be triggered by a number of things, including overexertion. Often SVT went away on its own. When I heard the doctor's reassurances, I felt relieved. But Cindy didn't. She became obsessed with her racing heart. It was all she talked about.

* * * * *

Jake agreed to put up the money—at least in part. As I sat with him and Ella at their kitchen table, he said that while he didn't think that we had a firm deal for the full amount, he felt ethically obligated to his initial commitment. He wrote a check.

Let's hope this works out, he said.

It will, I said.

How do you know? he asked.

I just believe it will, I said.

* * * * *

December arrived—we were nearing the critical December 5 release date. Mom was calling me more and more to see how things were coming. She seemed very nervous.

Sometimes I hesitated to tell Mom very much, because in her love she had a tendency to try to help. But this time, I told her what was happening. We were taking a big chance here, I said. It was going to be a very sharp change in direction—like a speeding bobsled coming into a tight turn.

What if it doesn't work? she asked.

Well, then, I don't know, I said. But please don't try to help, OK?

I won't, she said.

* * * * *

In the December issue I had written an editorial simply called "Why We're Moving to Subscriptions." It was one of the hardest things I'd ever had to write.

"Seasons change," I began. "Sometimes dreams do too."

I explained to readers how we couldn't go forward with this ad-dependent model. We hoped that people would subscribe individually—maybe even purchase Christmas subscriptions for their friends and family. They could subscribe in two ways: by going online or by mail.

On December 5, the online orders began to stream in, several hundred a day. On December 6, the mail orders began arriving as well—a growing pile of envelopes. The stack of orders on Mark's desk *looked* impressive, but was it enough? At the end of the first week, the tally had crossed five thousand—but then it began to slow. After two weeks, it became apparent; we weren't going to hit the needed ten thousand subscriptions.

Mark and I sat and looked at each other. The worst news wasn't that the stack of orders on his desk wasn't high enough. The worst news was that the stack of bills on his desk wasn't small enough. We were staring at a massive business debt—except that now, of course, we had no business.

* * * * *

Friday evening we went over to my parents' place for dinner. I had told them what had happened, and their faces hung with sympathy. While Cindy and Mom talked in the kitchen, I sat in the living room with Dad. He seemed unsure of what to say.

Yeah, he remarked, Mom was disappointed that she didn't get better news from Warren Buffet.

*Huh?* Dad's comment was completely out of nowhere. *Warren Buffett?*

What? I said.

Dad went quiet. I guess I shouldn't have said anything, he said.

Mom contacted Warren Buffett?

Your mother loves you, and she was just trying to help. She wrote him a letter, and he wrote her back.

I stormed into the kitchen. You wrote to Warren Buffett?

Mom was speechless. She looked at Dad as if to say, Why did you tell him?

Why would you do that? I pushed.

I know, Andy, she said, shaking her head. I'm so sorry. I just was trying to help.

What did you write?

I just told him that you had started a values-based magazine that he might be interested in. I sent him a copy of the magazine.

May I see the letter?

She left the room and came back. At the bottom of her letter, Warren Buffett had written a short reply. You're a good mom, he scrawled, explaining that he wouldn't be able to help because it was very difficult to succeed as a newspaper insert.

I tossed the letter on the counter and walked away.

*****

The next week I contacted the publishers of *Parade* and *USA Weekend*, Walter Anderson and Chuck Gabrielson. Both were sympathetic to our situation.

It's very difficult to make it in this arena, Anderson said.

You came a long way in a short time, Gabrielson said.

Neither were in a position to buy us out.

I e-mailed *Reader's Digest*. Nothing.

I read something in the news about the struggling Kmart wanting to re-establish its connection with its customers. I remembered my former Wal-Mart idea.

*Why not?* I thought. *We've got a lot in common with Kmart financially.*

I e-mailed Kmart corporate. That same day, a vice president wrote back. She was intrigued by my idea: a magazine-insert hybrid. She asked me to contact their media agency to talk. I ripped open my office door, calling the staff together. We had a chance here.

In less than forty-eight hours, with the frantic help of our design team, we had turned *The Front Porch* into a new publication: *Close to Home* (brought to you by Kmart). We overnighted the prototype to the media agency, requesting a conference call.

We're awfully busy with the holidays, said the executive. Can we do this later?

No, we really can't, I said. We have to do it now.

Well, OK, he said, clearly irritated.

The conference call was frosty at best. *Close to Home* looks interesting, he said, but we're not in a position to make a decision this quickly. I'm sorry.

I looked at our assistants, Jill and Jackie. It's probably time, I said, that we help find you some new jobs.

*****

Just before Christmas Cindy and I sat on our bed. She stared at me, curling her lip.

What is it? I said.

I'm late, she said.

We just looked at each other. There was no way this could happen right then.

In October, when things started to look tight, we had made some adjustments to our personal health insurance. Among other things, we dropped our maternity coverage. Someday we wanted to have another baby, but not right now.

Cindy bought a pregnancy test. It had been a few years since we'd done this little exercise together. In the past, we'd been filled with excitement. This time we felt scared to death.

Cindy emerged from the bathroom and laid the tester on the counter. We leaned forward on our elbows, waiting for it to turn. When it did, neither of us said anything at all.

# *Chapter 15*
# Boxes

While our population at home was about to expand, at work it was contracting. Within days of the crash, I was the only one left in the office. We'd released our support staff, Chris was teaching again, and Mark had moved back to his attorney's office to do work he didn't like very well. Now it was just me, day after day, doing whatever I could to somehow give us another chance.

For the past two months, as things looked bleak, Mark and I had decided not to take a paycheck, and my personal finances were now getting very tight. At any other time in our lives, Cindy could have picked up some extra nursing shifts, but between her racing heart and the little pregnancy surprise, she could barely function. I plundered my still-young retirement account to give Cindy and me a little breathing room while I tried to figure things out.

I knew that I was entitled to draw my back salary, but I felt uncomfortable with the idea. The business only had a little cash remaining, and we were staring at a six-figure debt. How could I take a salary? I consoled myself that, prior to the default, we had paid *all* of our bills. We were a reputable company that paid its bills. Then I remembered Mark once mentioning that we hadn't ever gotten an invoice from Curtis Publishing, the company that had sold us the Norman Rockwell artwork. The cost was seven hundred dollars. It had been several months since we had received the art; Curtis Publishing had probably long since forgotten. But it bothered me that we hadn't paid this bill. I wrote a personal check for seven hundred dollars and mailed it off. Maybe God would bless this small, painful gesture. Maybe an e-mail would come through or the phone would ring.

That same afternoon, the phone rang. It was Cindy. She was at the hospital. Her heart had started racing again at a state park forty-five minutes away, where she and the girls were spending the day with Cindy's parents, who were visiting from Maryland. She had requested another ambulance and was now at the emergency room in Lincoln. She said that she was feeling fine now. It just helped to be in the hospital. As I drove across town, I felt dizzy.

*****

As December dwindled, so did my hope and energy. Each morning I turned the key and walked into the quiet office, but often I just sat there, my head resting on my desk. It occurred to me that this image would make a good *Front Porch* cover. We could call it "Going Out of Business." It was interesting. Previously, when I'd seen a Going Out of Business sign at a store, I felt excitement. Going Out of Business meant deep discounts for me, the consumer. But forevermore I would feel deep sadness and empathy. Going Out of Business meant that someone was experiencing the death of a dream.

Reluctantly, I began to shift my sights from *The Front Porch* to ways I could actually make some money and provide for my family of—five. I thought about how I could word my résumé: thirty-one-year-old publisher—large failed magazine. I e-mailed two friends, Dick and Todd, who worked in communications at Florida Hospital in Orlando. Did they know of any work that might fit me? Dick wrote right back. Funny I should e-mail, he said. They needed someone to help write a book about natural health principles—water, fresh air, exercise, all that stuff. It would pay well.

I felt a mixture of gratitude for the work and absolute repulsion at the thought of doing anything but *The Front Porch*. The file drawers next to me were heavy with my blood, sweat, and tears. No, we hadn't raised enough money but I'd learned a *lot* about this business. We were told that we'd come a long way in a short time. *A long way in a short time.* Even Warren Buffet had told Mom how hard this business was, but against all odds, we had been making progress. We'd been climbing Mount Everest barefoot! And people loved our product! Was I just supposed to throw it all away and go write some book about natural health principles? Was all of this just a waste of everyone's time? Was it, God? Just a waste of time? Relenting, I decided I could force myself to do the health book while still pursuing the possibilities with *The Front Porch.* It would buy me a few months and put off the need to take another full-time job.

I looked around the office. I definitely didn't need this much space; I felt like a marble rattling around in a can. Maybe if our landlords could find another renter, they'd let us out of our lease. I could just work from home. I wandered through the offices, the conference room, and the lobby, surveying what was left. This was going to take some time. Along with my own materials and our business records, we still had several dozen boxes of *Front Porch* issues stacked against a wall. Moving out was going to be a big job, but I knew someone who would help me at a moment's notice.

* * * * *

Dad hadn't come into our offices very often, and I knew why. He didn't want to be in the way. This business was my thing, and he wanted to give me the space I needed. When Dad did come in, he always brought along a big box of doughnuts for everyone. This was just like him. He didn't like to impose, and the doughnuts provided cover.

When things had begun to look bleak, however, Dad came into the office more frequently and without the doughnuts. All the former inhibitions had faded. He knew what I was going through, and he wanted to be there for me. Mom told me that at night Dad just pulled the covers up over his head, groaning.

I phoned Dad. Will you help me pack up *The Front Porch*? I asked quietly. He drove right over.

Let's get this done all at once, pal, he said. I don't want you to have to come back here.

We carried box after box out of the office, passing each other on the sidewalk, not saying much. Most of the back issues of *The Front Porch* we heaved into the dumpster. The important boxes I took home to my garage. All of this had a familiar feel to it. For years after Dad's crash, a portion of his garage was filled with boxes from his failed business. Now I would have my own set of boxes.

# *Chapter 16*
# Winter

Cindy and I sat in the waiting room at the obstetrician's office. I couldn't believe we were here again.

When the receptionist called our name, she said we would need to pay that day because we no longer had maternity coverage.

Don't you just bill us? Cindy said.

No, we really need to have payment today. You can just pay on your way out.

Cindy looked at me.

We'll use the credit card, I said.

Cindy wiped at her eyes.

After the examination, we stopped at the window to pay. The receptionist said that our bill had been reduced by a hundred dollars. Another mom in the waiting room had seen Cindy crying, and she had written a check. Cindy sighed, deeply touched by the woman's loving gesture. I felt appreciative too. But I also felt another emotion rising—anger at this situation I'd gotten us into.

* * * * *

In the early days after the crash, I had felt numb more than anything else. In fact, several people had even commented how level, even peaceful, I appeared. To them, it seemed as though I was taking the business disappointment in stride; that I still had Cindy and the girls and that as long as we were together, everything would be OK.

On Christmas Day, Dad gave me an envelope with five hundred dollars and a note. "I've never been prouder of you than I am now," he wrote.

I knew Dad thought I was handling everything gracefully—much more gracefully than he'd handled his own crash. One day he took me out to lunch. As we ate, it seemed like he wanted to say something important.

You're about to enter a very difficult period, he said. Are you sure you're holding up personally?

I'm fine, I said.

OK, Dad said, pulling back. I just wanted to check.

Dad didn't try to say anything more, but one Friday evening, he brought something by our house.

Who was that? I asked Cindy.

It was your dad, she said. He said he burned a CD for you.

I put the CD in the stereo. It was a slow melody with simple words:

> Don't give up—someone really loves you.
> Don't give up—someone really cares.
> Don't give up—someone really loves you.
> And that someone is the Lord.

I knew why Dad hadn't stayed at the house. He didn't want to get emotional in front of me. I appreciated the song he had left, but I didn't show any emotion. I was still too numb.

* * * * *

Before long, though, Dad's words at the restaurant were proving prophetic. This *was* getting difficult, and I was really beginning to simmer.

*This really sucks,* I thought, as I sat in my basement office day after day. I had no workplace to go to—no hope in sight. I spent the days alternating between trying to revive the business and forcing myself to write about natural health principles.

Upstairs, Cindy was feeling worse and worse. She said she didn't feel like she could even take care of the girls the way she wanted to. She felt like she needed someone taking care of *her.* She'd been talking with her mom and dad on the phone. They were urging that we come out and live with them in Maryland while she got better.

Live with your folks? I said. In *that* little house?

Cindy's voice got forceful. It's what I want to do, Andy, she said. I can't go on like this.

*****

A few days later, I called Dad.

Cindy feels like she needs her mom to take care of her, I said.

She's got to get past this, Dad said. You need her right now.

Well, she can barely take care of herself. We're both completely empty.

What can we do to help?

Dad, we're selling our house and going to Maryland for a while.

No, you shouldn't do that.

Dad, I said, Cindy's dad is flying here this weekend.

Dad hung up.

*****

A week later, one of Cindy's friends, Stephanie, came by the house. She had put together special care packages for the girls, now at the ages of five and three, full of toys and games and books. By the time Stephanie arrived at our place, the girls were already seated in our minivan just a few feet away from the For Sale sign in our front yard.

Here you go, girls, Stephanie said, as she handed the girls their packages. You can enjoy these on your big trip.

Ally and Morgan were delighted. They had already gotten some presents the night before when they'd gone out to spend some special time with Grandma and Grandpa, and now they were getting *more* presents.

But the fun wasn't over! Twelve hundred miles later, the girls would get even *more* presents. Mimi and Papa had set out some stuffed animals on two little beds at their house in Maryland. Here, girls, Mimi said, pointing at a twin-sized mattress pad on the floor. This will be Ally's bed. And in *here*—right around the corner here—will be Morgan's bed. How does *that* sound?

It sounds funnnn! screamed the girls.

Great! said Mimi, smiling. Now come on out to the kitchen and have some soup!

I watched the girls scramble into the kitchen, where Cindy sat talking with her dad. Then I carried my suitcase into the guest room just a few steps away. In this house, everything was just a few steps away.

Dropping my suitcase on the floor, I sat down on *my* new bed. *Oh, yeah,* I thought, *this is going to be lots of fun.*

# Chapter 17
# The Desert

The first thing I did was order cable.

Ostensibly, I ordered cable so that I could have high-speed Internet service for my laptop. Cindy's parents, the Griffins, didn't have high-speed service at the tiny farm home where we were all now living, and since our bedroom was now my office as well, I *needed* Internet service. I was the publisher of a large national publication that was temporarily suspended, and I needed high-speed Internet to try to get it going again.

Getting cable Internet into our bedroom also meant we got cable TV. This seemed appropriate since most prison cells have cable TV. I watched a lot of TV in our one-hundred-twenty-day stay at the Griffins' place. I watched TV at night with Cindy after we had put the girls to bed, and sometimes I watched TV during the day when I needed a break from my work or my life. I suppose the low point with the TV was getting choked up while watching reruns of *Happy Days*. When the joy has vanished from your life, as it had from mine, you settle for joy wherever you can find it, even if it's a special moment with Richie and the Fonz. Also, that theme music can really get to you.

It had been years since I'd watched *Happy Days,* and seeing it again brought back a rush of memories from childhood. Back then I'd fly off the school bus with my saxophone and duffel bag and race up our long gravel driveway with our Great Dane, Thor, leaping along beside me. Out of breath, I'd burst in the front door—Hi, Mom—and dump my stuff in the hallway and put a couple of Pop-Tarts in the toaster and pour a glass of milk, and if

I timed everything perfectly, I'd be sprawled on the couch right at four o'clock when the *Happy Days* theme song started. "Sunday, Monday, Happy Days! Tuesday, Wednesday, Happy Days! Thursday, Friday, Happy Days! Saturday—what a day! Groovin' all week with you!"

*Happy Days* was, in fact, a happy show, and that's why I'd liked it so much as a kid. But now I liked *Happy Days* for another reason—because for thirty minutes a day, it reminded me of when I used to be happy myself. Those days now seemed like a world away. How had everything changed so quickly? How, in only a few months, had I gone from being an idealistic young entrepreneur to an angry middle-aged man?

When I looked in the mirror, I barely recognized myself. I saw a person filled with bitterness and even hate. For starters, I hated *The Front Porch*. I hated everything about it. Hated that I'd ever thought of it. Hated how much I loved it. Hated how it had humiliated me in front of everyone. I also hated being *here,* in this tiny farmhouse. The stupid thing was, this wasn't even Cindy's parents' *real* home. This was just a temporary home that happened to be on the property they had purchased so that they could build their five-thousand-square-foot dream home up on the hill. *Perfect,* I thought. *Just when my thirty-year-old wife needs her mommy to take care of her, her mommy happens to be living in the world's tiniest farmhouse. This was just great.*

Making things even worse, Cindy's dad was up early most every day, working on the dream home. Every morning he'd come creaking down the stairs outside our bedroom wall. Then he'd carefully pull our bedroom door shut, which had to be open at night or we had no ventilation, so that he wouldn't wake us up. Too late! I had already heard his footsteps—was already lying there wide awake, feeling guilty that I had absolutely no plans to go up on the hill and help him with the house today, just as I hadn't helped him yesterday. I had trudged up there in the snow a few times the first week, but then I'd quit altogether. I *hated* construction—I was absolutely terrible at it.

As a teenager, I had worked several summers at a lakeside resort owned by our neighbor, Orlo Gilbert. Usually I just mowed lawns and cleaned beaches, which I liked because I could listen to the Minnesota Twins baseball games through my headphones. But one summer, Orlo ruined everything by getting the big idea for us to build a garage for the Corvairs he collected.

About thirty minutes and several bent nails into the process, I realized how much I was going to hate building this garage. I much, much preferred mowing lawns, which took almost no mechanical ability. *This is going to be a long summer,* I thought as Orlo told me to hold the tape measure still.

Fortunately, I was rescued by Colonel Oliver North. That summer Colonel North was testifying to Congress about his role in the Iran-Contra affair. Orlo and I were both interested in Ollie North's televised hearings; in fact, Orlo told me that if I wanted to watch the hearings, it was OK if I came to work late. Really, he said, it's no problem. I was delighted at this offer. For the next several mornings, as Orlo pounded nails in the distance, I sat in our lake cottage, watching Ollie North testify, his lawyer whispering mysterious things through cupped hands into Ollie's ear. It was fascinating. Unfortunately, Colonel North's testimony ended all too soon, and he was followed by the much less exciting Rear Admiral John Poindexter. Watching Admiral Poindexter testify before Congress was even more miserable than building a garage, so I sauntered back over to Orlo's place and picked up my hammer. Oh, you're back already? said Orlo.

I never did get very good at construction, and at Cindy's parents' place I didn't need anything making me feel worse than I already did. So most of the day I stayed down in the bedroom, grateful that I actually had the book project to work on. In the morning, I'd stumble out of the bedroom carrying my towel, the loser son-in-law headed to the shower. Then I'd go back to my room and work on the health book and on trying to somehow revive *The Front Porch.* The only smile I put on all day was for the girls when we'd go outside to play for a while. Beyond that, I didn't have anything much to give to anyone.

Neither did Cindy. This racing heart thing, whatever it was, had turned her into a completely different person. All she wanted to do was to be with her mom. Together they made meals in the kitchen or sat on the sofa, Cindy's mom rubbing her feet, Cindy sniffling and crying. She didn't *want* to be this way, she told me. She didn't want to be so terrified about being alone with a racing heart that she could barely think of anything else. She didn't want to constantly feel as if she was dying—as if her heart was going to pound right out of her chest.

You're not dying, I told her blankly as we drove yet again to sit in the emergency room parking lot.

I *know,* Andy, she said. But don't you understand that it makes me feel better just to be close to the hospital?

Well, when do *I* get to feel better?

* * * * *

I knew there were ways to feel better, and at opportune moments, I felt the pull of many of them. I had never been a drinker, but for the first time in my life, I understood the appeal of drinking. For the first time, I got why people escaped to alcohol. But I really didn't want to start drinking, so, instead I turned to eating. I noticed that when I ate, I felt better. Sometimes in the evenings, I'd skip the nutritious supper Cindy's mom had made, and I'd drive over to Waynesboro, where I'd sit in the Hardee's parking lot with a big cheeseburger, onion rings, and a shake. For a while—just a little while—I felt good again. The emptiness, however, always returned in force—the deep void that now seemed to accompany me everywhere I went.

A couple of times I took longer trips—to Virginia Beach and to Charlotte to look around at some future job possibilities—to get away. It was on these trips that I felt the strongest pull to forego it all, to escape from my world for much longer than a cheeseburger. But somehow, the pull was too weak. Jake might have been right about the business—that it didn't have a strong enough foundation to make it. But that wasn't going to be true for me. I had a foundation. I might be confused and angry and miserable, but I'd still take these over the loss of my family. I wasn't quitting that easily. I was going to forge ahead, even if it meant utter and total humiliation.

The humiliation was the hardest part—the absolute embarrassment of failing in business and living with my wife's parents. *What a loser.* Once when I'd come back from town, Cindy's mom said that a friend of hers had called. The woman's daughter, Anna, had been a student of mine in Lincoln. Anna and Alison, another former student of mine, were here in town, and they wanted to see me. They were driving out this Sunday. I couldn't possibly have imagined anything worse. I liked both of these students. I enjoyed them in class, which was precisely the reason that I didn't want them to see me like this. I wanted them to remember me the way I was. That Sunday afternoon when I heard the former students pull in the driveway, I felt like hiding in the closet.

Sometimes friends called to see how I was doing. I noticed how they tried different approaches to get me to feel better. Some tried the perspective approach. They'd remind me that many people had it much worse than I had it. This wasn't helpful to me at all. I was *plenty well aware* that people had it worse. Was the knowledge of other people's pain somehow supposed to make me feel better? (What? There are people starving in Africa? Boy, do I feel great!) Well, it didn't. Pain was pain. The presence of pain in other people's lives didn't magically mean the absence of pain in mine. I was growing tired of people's glib solutions to how I was feeling.

One guy, however, seemed to get it. My editor friend in Washington, D.C., Cliff Goldstein, used to call all the time about the business. Now he was calling all the time about me.

How you doing, man? he'd ask me.

Not too great, I'd tell him.

I knew that outside of my own dad, Cliff probably understood how I felt as well as anyone. He knew what it was like to have a dream—to be so deeply invested in something you had created. In his twenties, Cliff, a gifted writer and agnostic Jew, had traveled through Europe writing a novel. The novel was everything to him; it *drove* him.

Cliff's journey took him to Israel, where a stunning series of experiences culminated in his conversion to Christianity. He was baptized in the Jordan River. On his return to the States, Cliff had tried to retain both his faith and pieces of his former life. He finally realized that he couldn't have it all. A Voice in his head kept telling him to burn his novel. So one night, he did. He said it made all the difference in his life.

I talked to Cliff about *The Front Porch*. I didn't want it to be a god in my life as the novel had been in Cliff's life. I felt that I was willing to give it up. But there was another aspect here: the business debt. I felt a responsibility for that.

Do you think I should give up *The Front Porch*? I asked Cliff one night.

No, I'm not saying you should necessarily do that, he said. But what you have to do is submit. You have to submit. You have to pray yourself into submission.

* * * * *

There was another who understood. One evening Cindy's dad brought me a stack of books he had read several years earlier, including a book called *Disappointment With God* by Philip Yancey.

I hadn't talked very much with Cindy's parents since we had arrived. Though I loved and respected them both, I was too embarrassed to be open with them. I also resented how they had urged Cindy to move in with them. I thought that our stay was hurting Cindy more than helping her—she had grown more and more dependent on her mom. And I didn't think that Cindy's parents truly understood what I was going through. One weekend Cindy's parents were both going to be away. I felt relieved. I badly needed some time alone with my own family—just the four of us waking up together, eating breakfast together, and spending the day together. I couldn't *wait* for this weekend. But no. Cindy's mom's brother, Uncle Marvin, was going to be in our area. Ever gracious, Cindy's mom told Uncle Marvin that he was welcome to stay at the house with us.

Are you kidding? I told Cindy. Doesn't your mom know we need a little time together alone?

Cindy started to cry. Again.

* * * * *

But when Cindy's dad handed me the stack of books, I remembered something. He had gone through his own desert experience. A few years earlier, he had been unfairly pushed out of an administrative position he loved. He knew how it felt to be broken and humiliated. I read these books and others like them, including a short book called *Secrets of the Vine* by Bruce Wilkinson. The book talked about the different stages in our personal and spiritual growth, including a stage called the pruning stage. This is the most painful stage, Wilkinson explained, but it's also the most beneficial. You will know when you're being pruned. You will also know when your time of pruning is over.

The words rang in my head: *You will know when your time of pruning is over.*

I desperately hoped this would happen soon. The longer I was here, the worse I was feeling. After a while, not even *Happy Days* made me feel better. I'd just lie on the bed in tears, begging God for joy and peace.

## *Chapter 18*

# Summer Grace

We left in early June, four months after we'd arrived. Now eight months pregnant, Cindy had been feeling a *little* better about her racing heart, and that was all I needed to get us out the door and down the road. I'd never packed the minivan so quickly in my life.

While we were in Maryland, I hadn't been able to look very seriously for jobs because I didn't know how long we'd have to stay there. Cindy was terrified about being alone, so how could we move somewhere with me at work all day? But as Cindy's condition had improved, I decided to look around. We had sold our house in Lincoln, and I didn't know of any jobs back there. Dad suggested that I call my alma mater, Southern Adventist University, near Chattanooga, Tennessee, to see if by chance, they had any teaching openings. My stomach turned at the thought.

First of all, I wasn't sure how I felt about working for an Adventist employer again. Spurred on by some friends who said they had studied themselves out of the church, Cindy and I had been grappling with some hard theological questions about our Adventist faith—including whether our unusual Jewishlike practice of resting on Sabbath was still intended for Christians. Did the Sabbath contribute to our faith in Christ or distract from it? Cindy and I spent hours studying and talking about this; ironically, it became our deepest point of personal connection during an otherwise distant period. With all of our questions, I wasn't sure I was ready to be an Adventist employee again.

Second, in case anyone had forgotten, I didn't really *like* teaching very much. I had left teaching never to return. I sighed. Teaching would at least allow me to be home with Cindy through the summer, and if need be, between classes. I grabbed my cell phone.

It's funny you should call, Andy, said Wilma McClarty, the English department chair and my former professor. We've just had someone leave.

I took the job: a three-quarter time position, teaching freshman composition only. It wasn't what I wanted to do, and it wasn't the pay we needed, but it was something.

At least we'd be in our own home again. A couple of weeks prior to our move, Ally and I drove down to Chattanooga and found a nice three-bedroom rental home. Dad had encouraged me to pick out something decent; he said he'd send us a check each month to help pay for it. Reluctantly, I accepted his offer, not really wanting my dad to support my own family.

*****

Early in the morning, the four of us headed down Interstate 81 in our two vehicles: Cindy and the girls in the minivan and me in my old Plymouth Laser without air conditioning. The day was scorching hot; to cool down I kept the windows open and plenty of ice on hand.

I had estimated that we could be in Chattanooga in about eleven hours, but Cindy had other ideas. Periodically, I would see her turn signal flashing. She'd pull off the interstate and head in a beeline for a hospital, just to be close. Prior to the trip, without my knowledge, she had mapped out all the major hospitals along our route.

By evening we had gotten within twenty minutes of Chattanooga. I was sweating through my clothes, but I knew that the sight of our rental home would ease a long day. Suddenly, I saw Cindy flip on the turn signal. *Oh, my word,* I thought. *Not again.* As she exited, I speeded up to be beside her, motioning for her to roll down the window.

What are you doing? I yelled.

I'm done for the day, she said. Let's find a motel here.

What? I said. We're only twenty minutes away!

I'm done, she said, shaking her head.

Why can't you go twenty more minutes? We're almost there!

I can't do it.

We found a motel. The girls swam, I steamed, Cindy cried.

Eight years earlier, we had, with giddy smiles, uttered the words *for better or for worse, for richer, for poorer, in sickness and in health.* Now we were living them.

* * * * *

The next morning we finished the journey, settling into a spacious and cool split-level. The girls ran up and down the stairs, squealing. At long last, it was just the four of us once again.

A few weeks later, it was five. Our third daughter arrived on a hot July evening, bawling up a storm, fitting right in. We gathered close in the hospital room, kissing her, kissing each other—a warm rain of love and affection between us all, the way it used to be.

We named her Summer Grace. It had been a long, hard winter.

# Chapter 19
# Healing

Cindy and I had both hoped desperately that our new life in Chattanooga would change everything and would bring us happiness once again. And in some ways, it did. We all adored our beautiful new baby, Summer Grace. Each new movement and facial expression brought a smile to our faces. This little rascal had technically been with us all winter, but now she was here in the flesh—our reminder that out of something so difficult can come something so wonderful.

We also loved our new rental house and our neighbors: a family of four with two little boys. In the front yard most every evening, Cindy sat on a blanket with Summer while I played capture the flag with the older kids. This was tremendously healing to my spirit. When you feel like the world is against you, it helps to hang out with people who actually think you're neat.

Still, I wasn't fully at peace yet. I felt uptight about moving to Chattanooga. I knew a lot of people here from my college days, and I didn't want them to see me—not like this, not like the failure that I was. One afternoon we went to the Department of Motor Vehicles to get our car registration and drivers' licenses. When I reached the head of the line, I was told that I needed additional paperwork. I walked back out to my car to get it. As I rifled through the glove compartment, I thought I saw someone I recognized walking in my direction. Sure enough. It was Eric Johnson from college. Eric had always been a really nice guy, and at any other time, I would have called out his name.

But I didn't want to be seen right then. My shirt was soaked through, and I knew how generally terrible I looked. Plus, I didn't want old friends seeing me driving the same car I had driven in college eleven years earlier. I quietly shut the car door and quickly walked back toward the bureau, looking down, rubbing my forehead. I heard a voice.

Do I know you?

It was Eric. He had seen me.

I sighed inwardly and put on a surprised smile.

Oh, hey, Eric! How's it going?

Great! How's it going with you?

*Do I know you?* he had asked. It was a fitting question. At this point I felt as if I barely knew myself. What had happened to me in such a short time? Why was I hiding from old friends in a parking lot?

I had hoped that starting a new life would restore my spirits again, but that wasn't happening. I was still very low. One particularly tough evening, I found the courage to phone another friend who lived here in Chattanooga—a high school buddy who now worked in medicine downtown. Calling John wasn't an easy decision, but I knew it was the right one. John, I said quietly, I'm having a hard time dealing with everything. Do you know of any good counselors I can talk to?

* * * * *

Cindy was having a hard time too. We had both hoped that she would feel normal again after the birth—maybe the pregnancy hormones had been the problem all along. They weren't. After the birth, Cindy's heart still had abnormal rhythms, and she was still terrified of being alone. She was still squeezing my hand when she felt like we were too far away from a hospital. One afternoon I walked in late to a staff meeting at school. I explained that I'd been at the ER with Cindy—her heart had been racing. The staff members expressed their anxious concern, but I waved it off. This happens a lot, I said.

That night I got a phone call from one of my new teaching colleagues, Marcus. He had heard how I'd described Cindy. He wondered if Cindy had the same thing he had—panic disorder. I handed the phone to Cindy. As she listened to Marcus, she glared at me.

Cindy had always been cautious about medication in general, and she seemed especially resistant to what Marcus was suggesting—that perhaps the problem wasn't her heart after all. Perhaps the problem was her mind. Marcus told Cindy that he had battled anxiety and panic attacks for many years—that the only thing that really helped him was seeing a psychologist and getting some anxiety medication.

Cindy despised this possibility. She insisted her problem was her racing heart. I'm not psycho, she repeatedly told me.

I was getting increasingly frustrated at Cindy. Here a friend was trying to help—and she was being flat-out stubborn.

One evening I came upstairs after push-mowing the backyard in the late-summer heat. When I walked into the kitchen to get some ice water, I saw Cindy peering down at the backyard. Some toys and balls were still lying in the grass. I had just kicked them out of the way as I mowed.

Aren't you going to pick up that stuff? she said.

No, I'm too hot right now, I said, sitting at the table.

Cindy rolled her eyes. Well, I would just think, she said, that you'd want to pick everything up. It seems that most men would want their yard to look nice.

I looked at Cindy. Had I just heard correctly? Was she really comparing me to most men because I hadn't picked up all the yard toys? Had she stopped to consider how she compared to most *women* right now? Most *women* weren't afraid to be home alone!

After some choice words, I got up to leave. On my way out, I grabbed an empty plastic baby bottle from the table. I flung it hard toward the floor where Cindy was standing.

I'd never been a violent person—I'd never done anything like this. But the truth was, when I saw the plastic bottle ricochet off Cindy's leg, I didn't mind that much. A two-ounce plastic bottle didn't *hurt*. Maybe my throwing it would get Cindy's attention. Maybe she'd see how serious I was about her getting help.

Cindy whipped around and let out the worst primal scream I'd ever heard. Then she stormed past me, walked out the front door, and drove away.

Shaken, I walked to the girls' room to see if they were OK. They must have heard the fight. What I saw made me feel ill—the girls looked perfectly normal.

Fighting had become our new normal.

Three hours later, Cindy came back in quietly. We just stood and looked at each other for a while. What had happened to us?

We sat on the sofa. I apologized for what I'd done—for how I'd scared her. Cindy apologized that she'd phoned her sister and told her that she had a violent husband.

You really did that? I said.

Well, yes I did, she said, cracking a slight smile.

We talked about the girls—how they needed us to be whole again. Our refusal to get help was not only hurting us, it was hurting them. Cindy said she knew what she needed to do. It was just hard. I'm not psycho, she said.

I know, I said.

Cindy agreed to talk with a cardiologist who understood anxiety disorders. Along with the right medication, he gave Cindy a fuller understanding of why her heart had probably started racing in the first place. Her life had spun into a perfect storm—financial uncertainty, unexpected pregnancy, and new questions about her religious faith. Her *heart* was racing uncontrollably because her *mind* was racing uncontrollably. But this anxious state was not the person Cindy was. This was not the true Cindy. She needed to be able to separate the two.

It was remarkable. Within weeks of taking medications for anxiety, Cindy was becoming her old self again—laughing in the morning, planning little outings with the girls, and making jokes about going caving alone. Her journey toward healing had begun with three words: I need help.

* * * * *

Mine had too. My counselor, Steve, was not only a Christian psychologist; he had also been a businessman. I told Steve everything—how my business had failed—how I had failed.

You have to be careful, he said, not to make them the same thing.

What? I said.

Your work and you. They're not the same thing. *You* are not your work. *You* are Andy.

I knew I was talking to the right guy.

When your work fails, Steve said, you have to be careful not to think that you're a failure. By the same token, you also have to be careful when your work goes well.

Why? I asked.

Because, he said, when you experience success in your work, the emotions you feel may get very close to the emotions of worship.

Steve's words hit me hard. They cut me to the core. Like a fish being filleted. Like a fisherman being filleted. Somewhere I heard waves crashing against the shore.

*Chapter 20*

# The Things of Peter

Sometimes I found myself thinking more about Simon Peter.

One thing that had always intrigued me about the John 21 passage was what Jesus meant by His question to Peter: "Do you truly love me more than these?" (verse 15).

I wasn't the only one who had wondered about this. For centuries, Bible scholars had debated what Jesus meant. The most common interpretation was that Jesus was asking, "Do you love Me more than the other disciples do?" This interpretation certainly seemed to make sense, given that Peter once previously boasted of his love for Jesus. "Even if all fall away on account of you," Peter had said, "I never will" (Matthew 26:33). But Peter did fall away. Perhaps that's why Jesus was asking this question.

But there was another possible interpretation. Some scholars suggested that with the words "Do you truly love me more than these?" Jesus might not have been asking Peter to compare his love for Jesus against that of the other disciples. He might have been asking Peter to compare his love for Jesus with his love for "these" things—perhaps the fishing gear and the greater life of fishing. Fishing, after all, had been Peter's longtime ambition and identity, and he seemed to have a hard time letting go of his former life and all that it entailed. For the first year or two he had been with Jesus, Peter had only been a part-time disciple. He continued to work what appeared to be a successful fishing business; he and his partners, James and John, had multiple boats and hired help.

In fact, it was while Peter was at work one morning that his new Rabbi acquaintance, Jesus, finally seemed to get his full attention. As Peter was rowing in from a long night of fishing, Jesus stood teaching on the lakeshore.

Jesus told Peter to row back out into the lake—to "put out into deep water, and let down the nets for a catch" (Luke 5:4).

Peter obliged, and when his nets began to break with fish, he reacted in a very interesting way. "He fell at Jesus' knees and said, 'Go away from me, Lord; I am a sinful man!' " (verse 8). Peter's guilt-filled response may have meant that he had drifted in his young relationship with Jesus, even to the point of apostasy. After all, why was he still out fishing all night—and probably sleeping all day—when he could have been ministering with Jesus? Indeed, this may have been the larger story of Peter's life. Given the close proximity of Peter's house to the local synagogue, it's possible that Peter was born to be a spiritual leader but had rejected this calling, perhaps to pursue his own ambitions.

There was certainly no question that Peter was viewed by those around him as a leader. When the local religious officials in Capernaum wanted to know if Jesus paid the temple tax, it was Peter who they asked about it. Everyone seemed to look to Peter, including his brother Andrew and partner John, who as former disciples of John the Baptist, had headed straight to Peter once they had discovered the Messiah. Interestingly, Peter wasn't at the Jordan River with Andrew and John. He was somewhere else, probably fishing or selling fish.

So central was the life of fishing to Peter that, time and again, Jesus met him at the subject. "Come, follow me," Jesus had invited his part-time disciples after the first big catch, "and I will make you fishers of men" (Matthew 4:19). Even after Peter became a full-time disciple, fishing was still in play. When the Capernaum officials questioned Peter at his lake home about the temple tax, Jesus sent Peter out fishing to get a coin from the mouth of a fish. Repeatedly, Jesus seemed to gently inquire whether Peter loved life with Him more than he loved life with the fish.

*****

Much more sobering is the fact that Peter's interactions with Jesus often revealed an ambition for power and perhaps wealth that Peter had dragged along with him from his days as a fisherman. Peter was so appalled when Jesus first forecast His own suffering and death that "Peter took him aside and began to rebuke him." In a surreal scene, Jesus responded with a powerful rebuke of His own: "Get behind me, Satan! You are a stumbling block to me; you do not have in mind the things of God, but the things of men" (Matthew 16:22, 23).

The devastation of this scolding would be felt by Peter only one other time—at Gethsemane. In the preceding hours, Jesus had been preparing himself for His death and had spoken about it at length. But Peter would hear nothing of it; his concept of the Messiah didn't include surrender, let alone death. This was not what he had signed up for.

When Jesus had begun the Passover meal by washing the disciples' feet, Peter was repulsed by the image. A teacher wasn't supposed to wash the grimy feet of his own disciples. "No," said Peter. "You shall never wash my feet." Only after Jesus said, "Unless I wash you, you have no part with me," did Peter permit it (John 13:8).

When the detachment of soldiers and high priests entered the Garden of Gethsemane to take Jesus away, it was Peter who again pushed his own plans—drawing his sword and cutting off the ear of the high priest's servant. But rather than words of praise from Jesus, Peter heard harsh words of rebuke. "Put your sword away! Shall I not drink the cup the Father has given me?" (John 18:11). Again Jesus scolded Peter for having in mind the things of men—the things of Peter.

Against this background, the mind-set of Peter when he disowned Jesus becomes more clear. What was the real reason that Peter told the servant girl that he wasn't a disciple of Jesus? Was it because he was afraid? Probably not. If Peter was afraid for his own life, why would he have drawn his sword among Roman soldiers?

There was a more likely explanation for why Peter said he wasn't a disciple of Jesus: he no longer *saw* himself as a disciple of Jesus. In his deep confusion about Jesus' apparent march to death, Peter didn't know who He was. He shouted, "I don't know the man!" *because he didn't know the Man* (Matthew 26:72).

* * * * *

The driving issue in Peter's life wasn't how he stacked up against the other disciples. The issue was how his plans stacked up against Jesus' plans. This was his biggest point of weakness. Jesus knew this, and it's why He had told Peter at the Passover meal, "Simon, Simon, Satan has asked to sift you as wheat. But I have prayed for you, Simon, that your faith may not fail. And when you have turned back, strengthen your brothers" (Luke 22:31).

In Peter's day, the sifting of wheat was a violent act used to separate the grain from the stalk and the chaff. It literally ripped the wheat apart. In the spiritual sense, writes Bible teacher Beth Moore, sifting is

> an all-out onslaught by the enemy to destroy you and cause you to

quit. It surfaces what you detest most in yourself and reveals the ugliness of self. . . .

Satan's goal in sifting is to make us a mockery by showing us to be all chaff and no wheat. Christ, on the other hand, permits us to be sifted to shake out the real from the unreal, the trash from true. The wheat that proves usable is authentic grain from which Christ can make bread.[1]

Peter wasn't the only one who would be sifted. When Jesus said, "Satan has asked to sift you as wheat," the word *you* was plural. All the disciples would be sifted in their own way, including Judas, who was found to be without any spiritual grain at all. But Peter's story would be different.

The third time that he denied that he was a disciple of Jesus, Jesus Himself "turned and looked straight at Peter" (Luke 22:61). The original Greek word for "looked straight at" is *emblepo.* This same word was used to describe the way Jesus looked at Peter when they first met. The word means "to see with the mind, to understand." And what Jesus saw in Peter—blended with all the chaff of pride, selfishness, and personal ambition—was the grain of faith.

1. Beth Moore, *Jesus: 90 Days With the One and Only* (Nashville, Tenn.: B & H Publishing, 2007), 375.

## *Chapter 21*

# One More Try

Steve had been right. The business had completely taken over my emotions. When the business was up, I was up. When the business was down, I was down. It had become an idol to me. But not only that—my idol and I were taking my family up and down along with us. When Cindy's psychologist explained that Cindy's heart problem really wasn't a heart problem but rather an anxiety problem, I felt the weight of responsibility even more. Deep down, I had feared this all along—that my business risk had pushed Cindy over the edge. The more I recognized what had happened, the more I despised the business and never wanted to spend another minute working on it. Had it been just me, I would have gladly left it all behind.

But that was the problem. It wasn't just me. What I couldn't seem to shake, like an albatross around my neck, was how this venture had affected so many others as well. On this point Cindy agreed with me. She has a strong moral compass, and she, too, was bothered by how the business had left others hanging.

First, there were the investors. Sure, they understood the risks they were taking, but that didn't really matter. These people had put their trust in me. Joe's words rang in my head. *Andy,* he'd told me after we'd cut the deal, *I'm doing this because I believe in you.* The fact that Joe was wealthy didn't make much difference to Cindy and me. A man had shown confidence in me, and I had let him down. We also felt sympathetic toward Jake and Ella. They weren't rich people; Jake had worked hard for many years to put that money aside. Publicly I showed them only bitterness, but privately Cindy and I grieved their loss.

But the people who haunted us most were the creditors. I often thought of the specific people whom we hadn't been able to pay, like the woman at the small stationery store to whom we owed two thousand dollars. Her words rang in my head too: *We've never had an unpaid bill like this before.* It was these creditors that drove me. I may not have been the savviest businessperson in the world, but I knew right from wrong, and I was going to do everything possible to make this right.

*****

But how to do it? In Maryland I had stared out that bedroom window many long hours, desperately trying to figure out a way to restart the business—with barely any money. I'd certainly learned a few things from the previous year.

First, I'd learned the importance of a secure foundation. It wasn't enough to have a great idea; you had to allow enough time for others to discover your great idea. You needed plenty of *space* in your budget. My friend Todd in Orlando had given me a book called *Great Failures of the Extremely Successful.* It told the same story over and over—people with too much vision and not enough resources. Most millionaires, the book said, had previously gone bankrupt an average of two or three times. This both astonished me and made me feel better. Even Joe had once told me that it took him seven years to figure out how to make any money. I'd noticed how carefully Joe had buffered his own investment by setting up several layers of corporations—so that nothing could touch his personal wealth. I'd learned how important a foundation was—a house built on a rock.

Second, I'd also learned the value of a dollar. It now made perfect sense to me why, as I'd read, the Wal-Mart executives slept in cheap motels. Once you learn how to spend money carefully, it's very hard to get out of that mind-set. While our office work flow had been pretty efficient, I'd made a few errors. For example, by paying authors so much, we were glutted with submissions—which took too much of our time.

Third, I'd learned a subtle but important lesson about sales: eagerness can be a turnoff. When you act too eager in business, people tend to pull away. They get nervous by what they perceive as your desperation. You've got to be careful to appear that you're not flying by the seat of your pants, that you don't appear to be negotiating out of fear. It helps if you really aren't.

Along with the lessons learned, I still had one quality of my own: perseverance—a refusal to give up. For whatever reason, perseverance came naturally to me. When I was a kid learning to water-ski, Dad had always said I shouldn't be afraid to fall. Falling, he said, is the only way you get better.

I had fallen hard. It was time to get up again.

* * * * *

In October 2003, ten months after we'd suspended production, *The Front Porch* returned. Through all those lonely months, I'd come up with a new model that would cost very little and possibly generate profit from the start. We'd provide *The Front Porch,* not as a preprinted monthly magazine, but as a weekly predesigned feature, delivered electronically, that would fill a page in the newspaper. We wouldn't charge newspapers anything for the feature. Instead, we'd sell national advertising into a portion of the page. Since we no longer had printing costs, we could sell ads at low rates and still make money. While in Maryland, I'd twice gone to meet with the publishers of the *Washington Times*. They agreed to sign up for this modified product. After months of calling and e-mailing, so did about forty more newspapers. It wasn't the flashy full-color product and the large circulation we'd had before. But it was something.

After class each day in Chattanooga, I worked on *The Front Porch* from our third bedroom, which I shared with Summer. I put together the content myself; I sold the ads myself. From Lincoln a former student worker, Pauline, assisted me with the rest of the operations. Dad helped me with the books. Neither Dad nor I took any pay. Our pay came in the form of our first monthly statement; *we were turning a profit.*

I would receive pay in one other form—in an article that appeared in a small newspaper in northern California. It was written by Debra LoGuercio, the single mom who had won our national columnist search. We had suspended just before we could announce Debra to the country. Debra was devastated—but not angry. Through the months Debra had written to me often, seeing how things were going, encouraging me personally. When we resumed our operation, we finally announced Debra as our columnist. In her own local newspaper column, she wrote about it.

If you've been reading this column long enough, you know that it was about this time last year when I was finally given the go-ahead from *The Front Porch* editor to announce that I'd won their nationwide columnist search. This was my dream come true: national syndication, and hopefully, hopefully, hopefully, an income someday that would allow me to do all my work at home in my PJs before noon and spend the rest of the day poolside, polishing my toenails. When *The Front Porch* picked me to be their columnist, it was the first step toward making that dream a reality. And I was walking on air.

But then I stumbled. Hard. Wound up with strawberry burns on both knees. Just as the first issue featuring my column was to appear in *The Front Porch,* the publication lost a key piece of financial backing. There just wasn't enough money to continue publishing this darling little fledgling magazine, devoted to average American life. That issue with my first column never made it to press. In show business, they'd say the play closed before it opened.

*The Front Porch* editor and publisher, a wonderful guy named Andy Nash, didn't give up on his own dream, however. . . . Last summer, just when I least expected it, I got an e-mail from Andy asking if I was still interested in writing for *The Front Porch.* I lost track of how many exclamation points I typed after the "Yes!" in my response.

Andy's determination to make his dream come true, to find a window when life closes a door, reminds me of a bumper sticker I saw the other day: Keep failing until you succeed. The only guarantee for failure is to stop trying.

# *Chapter 22*
# Club of the Broken

The first few months of the relaunch were going great. We were selling ads, recruiting newspapers, and best of all, making money. I even began mailing repayment checks to our creditors. The woman at the stationery store in Lincoln was shocked to hear from me again, let alone get a check for the full two thousand dollars. It was a fantastic feeling to be headed in the right direction. Dad celebrated along with me.

I'd also gotten a tremendous boost of encouragement in the form of a phone call.

Yeah, is this Andy Nash? said a voice I hadn't heard before.

Yes, it is, I said.

Andy, this is Frank Lalli calling from *Reader's Digest*.

I couldn't believe it. Months earlier, I'd e-mailed *Reader's Digest,* attaching a sampler of *The Front Porch,* on the random chance they might be interested in acquiring us. Frank Lalli was a vice president at *Reader's Digest.* He had previously been a senior editor at *Time,* managing editor at *Money,* and editor-in-chief of *George* after John F. Kennedy Jr. was killed in a plane crash. He'd once been named America's editor of the year. He was calling *me?*

Frank said that he was impressed with *The Front Porch.* He said that if they were starting *Reader's Digest* again today, they would do it much the same way. I was blown away. A big-time editor like Frank Lalli actually liked my work? I felt like Rudolph the red-nosed reindeer after Clarice said she liked him—"She said I'm cute! She said I'm cute!"

In November I flew to New York to meet with Frank. Though *Reader's Digest* didn't acquire *The Front Porch* itself, the affirmation from Frank meant a great deal to me at a time when I had begun to question my own ability. His words gave me the encouragement I needed to press on.

*****

Just before Christmas, I got another phone call. I didn't recognize the number and hoped it might be a new client. Is this Andy Nash? said a voice.

Yes, it is, I said hopefully.

The caller identified himself as an attorney with a collection agency on behalf of Quebecor World printing.

Are you aware, he said, that you've got a past due balance in six figures?

Yes, I am, I said. We're working to get that paid down.

It's twelve months past due, he said.

I know, I said. But we had an unexpected shortfall, and it's taking some time to get back on our feet.

Well, it's taking too long, the man said angrily.

I didn't say anything.

You're aware, he said, that you're the personal guarantor for this balance?

What? I said.

You signed your name as personal guarantor.

What do you mean?

When you set up credit with us, you signed that you would personally back any outstanding debts.

I felt dizzy. What was going on? Personal guarantor? My mind scrambled. I vaguely recalled some paperwork when we'd set up our account a year and a half earlier.

The collection agent's voice brought me back.

You can forget about that new car you want to purchase.

Huh? I don't want to purchase a new car.

Well, you can forget about it, he said.

I regained my composure.

Look, I said, I've been working for twelve months without pay to do the right thing here. I'm not doing this because I'm a guarantor for this debt. I'm doing this because it's the right thing—period. And I don't need you or anyone else calling to *motivate* me.

The man softened. Hey, I'm just doing my job, he said.

I hung up the phone and put my head on the desk.

*****

This wouldn't be the only time I felt the strange new sting of being talked down to. After a year of renting, Cindy and I decided to buy a modest house nearby. The house payment would be lower than our rental payment, so it made sense for us. When we'd bought our previous house in Lincoln, we sailed through the process. I had great credit and solid W-2 employment.

At first the mortgage broker sounded positive and told us to go ahead and pay for the home inspection. But when he reviewed our paperwork from the previous haywire year, he changed his tone. He called and said he couldn't help us. Certain that he was misunderstanding our information, I drove over to his office and sat in the lobby. His assistant told him that I was waiting, but more than an hour later, he hadn't come out. When he finally did come out, he walked right past me without saying a word. I felt humiliated.

Without warning, I was getting a little taste of how it felt to be a second-class citizen. This was how a lot of people felt *all* the time, I realized. It was enough to rob you of your will to keep trying. As painful as this was, I sensed that somehow this experience would ultimately be valuable for me. I had a good education—someday I would be back on my feet. I wouldn't always be driving around in ninety-five-degree heat in a beat-up car without air conditioning. I wouldn't always need Dad to send us a check each month to help pay our bills. Someday things would be better again. In fact, they were already getting better—we found a different mortgage broker who helped us buy the house.

But I thought about the people who couldn't count on their lives being better: the truly down-and-out without a family member to bail them out when needed. With shame I remembered a thought I'd once had. When I was only ten or eleven, I had been thinking about poor families I'd seen standing outside shabby, stifling houses. Suddenly, I got an idea that made me feel better. The mall! People who lived in poverty could go to the mall!

The mall had a clean, fun environment—and it had air conditioning! Poor people could go sit at the mall!

It had been a ridiculous way to make myself feel better. Sure, I was only a kid, but how much had I really moved past this insensitive mind-set? Getting blasted by a collection agent, getting rejected by a mortgage broker—these types of experiences had at least partially sensitized me to those who had it much, much worse. In a strange way, I was becoming grateful for my desert experience, and periodically, I ran into others whose eyes had been opened as they trudged through the sand.

One hot summer evening at the girls' Little League game, I noticed two people that I hadn't seen in years. In college, Bob and Michelle had been the quintessential dream couple: smart, outgoing, good looking, and athletic. Bob and Michelle had the world by the tail and seemed set for a bright future. But on this evening, something in their countenances seemed different to me. I walked over and said Hello.

Oh, hey, Andy, they said quietly—without the confidence I remembered.

What have you two been up to? I said.

Bob and Michelle stole a glance at each other, both of them seeming to sigh. They began to tell me about opening a bicycle shop in Orlando—a dream they shared. Before they even finished, I knew what had happened. Things hadn't worked out. It was almost as though I could sense the despair in their souls—the sand in their hair. At that moment, I realized that we were all part of the same club—the club of the broken. There was a specialness to our conversation, a deep empathy that we shared. To be able to talk to someone who understood was deeply meaningful. It was then that I recognized the gift I'd been given—the ability to empathize with others who were broken. More than ever before, I would be able to say, I understand.

The experience gave me new insight into the Incarnation. Christ, too, had joined the club of the broken. The only difference was, He had chosen to join.

* * * * *

One evening Dad called. Grandma Nash was getting up in years and had decided to stop driving. She wanted to know if I would be interested in her old Buick Park Avenue.

Sure, I said. Hey, Grandma's Buick wasn't exactly the most sporty car, but at least it had air conditioning. Dad said he'd drive it out from Colorado when he got a chance.

I decided to see what I could get for my old Plymouth Laser. I took it to a Wednesday night car auction. The auction was a safe way to try to sell your car. You could set a reserve price with the auctioneer, and if you didn't get your price, you could just drive home. Before the auction started, I noticed a teenager and his father checking out my car in the evening shadows. They sat in the car, walked around it, then sat in it again. The kid really seemed excited about the car. I was reminded of how excited I was about this same car when my own dad and I discovered it fourteen years earlier. I walked over to the car.

Are you the owner? the teenager asked me.

Yes, I said.

How much are you hoping to get for this car?

I'd like to get a thousand, I said.

The kid's face fell.

Well, he said, if you don't get a thousand at the auction, will you take five hundred for it afterward?

Oh, I don't know, I said. I'll have to see.

The auction brought bids from several parties. I noticed the teenager drop out at five hundred dollars, and then the used car dealers took over. When the bidding stopped at seven hundred dollars, the auctioneer turned to me. Did I want to accept? I shook my head No. I had decided what I wanted to do.

The car rolled on through, and I followed it back to the holding area. The teenager and his dad trailed behind. I told them to meet me at the gas station on the corner. We weren't allowed to do private business at the auction itself.

At the gas station, I pulled out the car title. The teenager smiled at his dad. He was about to buy his first car. When we finished filling out the title, the teenager pulled out his checkbook. I stopped him.

I want you to have the car, I said. It was given to me, and now I want to give it to you. You can use your money to fix it up a little.

The teenager just looked at me, dumbfounded. The joy on his face was worth much more to me than five hundred dollars. As I watched him drive away, it was the best I'd felt in a long, long time.

# *Chapter 23* Hero

Day after day, month after month, I kept chipping away at the six-figure debt. Increasingly weary and lonely, I wished I could just get the monkey off my back once and for all.

I came across a profile in *Investor's Business Daily* about Richard Newcombe, the president of a very successful publishing company, Creators Syndicate. Like me, Newcombe had had a very difficult earlier experience in publishing. Eleven months into his operation, his company was "hemorrhaging tens of thousands of dollars a week and bankruptcy was just months away." But Newcombe refused to give up.

"I mean I really had it in my head," he said later, "that if I had to, I'd crawl over broken glass. I'd live in a tent—it was gonna happen. And I think when you have that kind of steely determination—sort of like Margaret Thatcher or Winston Churchill—people get out of the way." Newcombe's fortitude helped position his company as a legitimate player in the syndication market, and it caught the attention of leading advice columnist Ann Landers, who was then writing for another syndication company. Newcombe was able to attract Ann Landers as a client, which suddenly gave Newcombe's company twelve hundred additional newspapers—a whopping amount of weekly revenue and the kind of credibility he needed. His company never looked back.

I resonated with Richard Newcombe. I knew how it felt to be willing to crawl over broken glass to make the business work. I also knew that if I could retain just one major client, such as Ann Landers, we could pay off our debts once and for all—and maybe start paying back our investors as well. I knew the client I wanted.

*****

Ever since childhood, I had felt proud that the funny guy on the radio, Garrison Keillor, was a Minnesotan just like me. I had never actually read Keillor's books, however, until my volunteer year in southern Thailand. On one of our weeklong breaks, Jeff and I decided to spend a week in Singapore: a twenty-two-hour bus ride away. Prior to our departure that morning, Jeff said he was packing a few peanut-butter sandwiches for the trip in case there wasn't anything good to eat at the bus stops.

You'd better make some too, he told me.

Nah, I said. There will be something along the way.

I couldn't have been more wrong. Every bus stop through Malaysia either had no food for sale—or no food that I could possibly bring myself to eat. By evening, I was ravenously hungry. As it was getting dark, I noticed Jeff turn toward the window. He seemed to be unwrapping something. I thought I could hear crinkling. Yes, it was definitely crinkling. It was the *sandwiches.* Pressing himself against the window, Jeff tried to surreptitiously gulp down a sandwich without my noticing. I was livid. How could he sit there eating peanut-butter sandwiches when I was sitting here starving? Did he honestly think I didn't know what he was doing?

As he quietly chewed, Jeff looked visibly torn between sharing his sandwiches and taking an attitude of I told you so. His paper bag crinkled some more. Finally, Jeff quietly said, Here, guy, why don't you have one of these?

Forget it, I said. I can tell you don't even want to share.

No, go ahead, he said weakly, holding out a sandwich.

I took it and muttered, Thank you. We sat there in the dark, eating our sandwiches in the middle of Malaysia, not realizing how hysterically hard we and our wives would laugh at this incident, years later.

On the bus trip back to Thailand, I brought plenty of food, which I graciously offered to Jeff. Even better, I had found treasure in a Singapore shopping plaza: a copy of *USA Today* and a book, *Lake Wobegon Days* by Garrison Keillor. As soon as I began reading *Lake Wobegon Days,* I knew that the book would be over far too soon, so I limited myself to just one chapter a day. I loved the way Garrison Keillor wrote about growing up in Minnesota. One of my favorite stories was the time he described playing softball against his intimidating uncle Earl:

> When I was fourteen, he came up to bat one hot July afternoon in the Father-Son softball game and looked at me playing third base and pointed his bat at me. I crouched; my mouth was dry and my heart pounded. He waited for a low pitch and drove it straight down the baseline—a blazing swing, a white blur, a burst of chalk dust—I drove to my right just as the ball nicked a pebble—it bounced up and struck me in the throat, stopping my breath, and caromed straight up in the air about fifteen or sixty-five feet. Blinded by tears, I hit the ground face first, getting a mouthful of gravel, but recovered in time to catch the ball, and kneeling, got off a sharp throw in the vicinity of first which caught him by a stride. I was unable to speak for twenty minutes. That play was some proof that I was all right. Everyone saw it and said it was great; even guys who didn't like me had to say that, because it was.[1]

In the world of writing, Garrison Keillor became an immediate hero to me, and when I returned to the States, I read all the books and articles I could find. One winter evening, he came to Washington, D.C., to do a book signing. Cindy and I carried our three-month-old, Ally, through the cold night air to see him. As Garrison Keillor signed our books, he kept looking fondly at Ally, even leaning down to her car seat in which she was sleeping. I later learned the reason: he and his wife were expecting their own baby girl a few months later. After Garrison Keillor signed my book, he let Cindy take a picture of him and me together. I could barely speak.

Four years later when we'd launched *The Front Porch,* I e-mailed *Prairie Home Companion,* requesting an interview. That same day Garrison Keillor replied to me personally, saying that he would be glad to do the interview but requesting that we do it via e-mail; he explained that he tended to ramble in spoken interviews. That was fine with me—I was worried that I would ramble too. Later that week, I e-mailed my questions to Garrison Keillor's personal e-mail account, and he gave me some hilarious answers, which we published in *The Front Porch.*

* * * * *

As I thought about what person could give *The Front Porch* the Ann Landers–like boost it needed, who could be better than Garrison Keillor? Sure, he was a celebrity, which we typically avoided, but he was a different kind of celebrity. He was one of us.

I wrote to *Prairie Home Companion* with an idea. Since I'd noticed that Keillor was already doing a light question and answer (Q&A) style column on his Web site, how about allowing *The Front Porch* to pick up some of this material, package it as a weekly column, and market it to newspapers? Keillor's representative, a woman named Amanda, responded and said that she was intrigued with the possibility. In fact, she had talked preliminarily with Garrison, and he sounded OK with it.

Yes! This was a promising break. I immediately contacted a sampling of newspaper editors around the country to see if they'd be interested in a Q&A humor column by Garrison Keillor. The response was immediate and overwhelming. The newspaper editors *loved* the idea. I did the math. Extrapolating the newspaper sampling to the total number of newspapers in the country, I estimated that right off the bat, at least four hundred newspapers would be willing to order the weekly Garrison Keillor column. That would be a fantastic initial number. Even after paying Garrison Keillor his share, we would make $3,000 a week, $13,700 a month, and $156,700 a year in straight profit. We'd be able to quickly pay off our debts and start paying the investors. This was amazing!

Over the next few weeks, Amanda and I corresponded about the finer workings of the arrangement—and then she asked for the contract itself. She said she'd try to get it signed and returned by that Friday or the following Monday.

Early Friday afternoon, Amanda called.

I feel ill, she said.

What do you mean? I said.

Something has happened, she replied. Garrison has been contacted by a large syndication company that would like him to write a column. He says he wants to explore this.

I went quiet. It was almost as though I knew something like this would happen.

Doesn't he know about *The Front Porch*? I said.

Yes, he does, Amanda said. And the thing is, in my heart I know this is right. But it's his call. The other column wouldn't be a humor column. It would be a current events or political column—something like that.

Is there anything I can do?

I would suggest, she said, that you write him a letter today. E-mail it to me, and I'll make sure he gets it.

That afternoon I sat at my laptop and nervously wrote a personal letter to Garrison Keillor. I told him about all the work we'd already done—that everything was set. I told him that newspapers loved the idea of a Q&A humor column. I told him that I was a Minnesotan too.

I e-mailed the letter to Amanda's account and waited. The next week I called. Amanda said that she didn't know anything yet. She seemed more flustered than before.

Finally, still having his e-mail address from our previous interview, I nervously e-mailed Garrison Keillor himself.

"Mr. Keillor," I wrote,

> certainly you have the right to do what you wish with your own words. The problem is that, based on what we had been told, we really went forward in total good faith, and I personally don't believe that a company like yours would leave us hanging after all our work. (I feel as though you might not be aware of the scope of all this.) . . . We've got all these contacts with newspapers that literally are asking us when the Keillor column will be available. We have no idea what to say at this point.
>
> Will you give us this opportunity? We've prepared for this and will work hard to bring you as many newspapers as possible.

That same day Garrison Keillor replied. "Mr. Nash," he wrote,

> it's a simple question that has to be faced right now: does [this] material hold up as general-interest material for publication? You say it does and in your enthusiasm you've generated interest among newspapers, based on our interest in the idea. Now we are facing the cold hard reality of the thing: do we want this Q&A column to go out as an independent endeavor? . . .

I am 62 years old, and that's old enough not to get talked into writing something I don't think I can write. You can give me the bum's rush if you wish, but frankly I don't appreciate it.

I read Garrison Keillor's letter only once. It was too painful to read it twice.

---

1. Garrison Keillor, *Lake Wobegon Days* (New York: Viking Penguin, 1985), 187.

*Chapter 24*

# Going the Distance

There wasn't going to be a quick solution to our huge business debt. I was going to have to do this the hard way. Each day after teaching my composition classes, I came home and climbed the stairs to the main headquarters, where I edited articles, sold ads, and phoned newspapers asking if they'd like to start carrying *The Front Porch,* a wholesome, fun feature that celebrated ordinary people, not celebrities.

Three years after we'd relaunched, in the fall of 2006, I mailed off a large settlement check to our printer, paying off the debt obligation. It was a fantastic feeling. In fact—and this shocked me—paying off this debt was an even *better* feeling than going into business in the first place. I felt a tremendous sense of accomplishment that I had stuck to this. No, I hadn't succeeded as a magazine publisher, but I felt like I had at least succeeded as a person.

The past few years of the business had been very different from the first year. The first year was all about making a big splash, fulfilling a personal dream, even getting rich. The first year was about me. The past few years hadn't been like that at all; they were about persevering, about ethics, about others. Though I was now able to take some pay and still had faint hope that the business would grow to the point that I could do it full time again, this hope wasn't what kept me climbing the stairs to my home office all those evenings. It was a desire to do the right thing.

* * * * *

My favorite movie growing up was *Rocky*. I was captivated by the story of the down-and-out Philadelphia fighter given the opportunity to fight the champ, Apollo Creed. Everyone knew that Rocky had no a chance at winning; the title fight was an exhibition, a symbol, a joke. But it wasn't a joke to Rocky. Though overmatched on paper by Apollo's strength, speed, and stature, Rocky had one attribute in his favor: his heart. And it was from his heart where he drew his strength.

As a boy, on the living room floor, I had trained along with Rocky—imitating his signature one-arm push-ups. As I got older, I began relating to *Rocky* for other reasons, not for the boxing itself but for Rocky Balboa's sheer determination, his resolve to show himself well; and to the struggling actor, the young Sylvester Stallone, refusing to sell his *Rocky* script unless he could play the lead.

At the close of the original *Rocky* movie, Rocky steps into the ring with Apollo Creed. No one expects Rocky to last even a few rounds, but he hangs in. Round after round, Rocky takes a beating from Apollo, withstanding his hardest licks, getting in a few of his own. Near the end of the fight, Apollo unleashes a devastating uppercut that hurls Rocky to the floor. The fight is over—but no! He's struggling to get up. Somehow Rocky finds his footing and beckons for more. Apollo can't believe it. When the final bell sounds, Rocky is still battling toe to toe with Apollo. The two warriors have to be pulled apart. Rocky hadn't won the fight, but he had shown himself well. He had gone the distance.

*****

In December 2006, shortly after I mailed the check, our family took a holiday road trip to the East Coast to see Cindy's family. We stayed in their spacious new home, which I'd helped build for approximately twenty-eight minutes, up the hill from the tiny farmhouse we'd all inhabited nearly four years earlier. We never really talked much about our long winter together. Whenever the subject pushed itself to the surface, we just smiled and shook our heads and let it sink back down again. I loved Cindy's family, and they loved me, too, but some periods of life were better left unspoken.

After a few days in Maryland, Cindy and I decided to take the two older girls, Ally and Morgan, to New York City to experience the holiday rush.

Three-year-old Summer stayed behind with Cindy's parents. The quickest route to New York was Interstate 81 through central Pennsylvania, but as I studied the atlas, I felt a secret motivation to somehow go east about a hundred miles.

Hey, I said as we drove, if we cut over on Highway 30, we can drive through Amish country.

Oh, that would be fun, said Cindy, her eyes as bright as they used to be.

Yeah, I said, then we can just swing through Philadelphia and catch the toll road north.

You want to run up the *Rocky* steps, don't you? she said.

It was quiet for a moment. We're so close, I said.

Cindy laughed. While she wasn't a big *Rocky* fan, she knew it was important enough for me to run the steps just once in my life.

We pulled up to the Philadelphia Museum of Art about seven o'clock that night. It was already getting dark, but the actual setting was more impressive than I'd expected. The run itself was even better. With Cindy taking a video, I started running from the park, the way Rocky did, with Ally and Morgan trailing. I punched the air in front of me, then beckoned the girls behind me, Come on! Come on! I said, as they giggled. We ran past the *Rocky* statue at the foot of the steps. Then, picking up speed, we began ascending the famed steps where Rocky Balboa first ran to "Gonna Fly Now," when no one thought he could fly but him.

There are seven steps in the final flight, and in the movie, Rocky carries them in just two steps. I was determined to do this. I didn't want to take three steps; I wanted to take two. With a big run-up, I leaped to the fourth step, landing on my left foot, and then with a burst of willpower, managed to lunge to the top. To my surprise and delight, I even grunted like Rocky did. It was as close to a perfect moment as I'd had in a long time.

By the time Ally and Morgan caught me at the top, I was already shouting things like We're gonna win! and Adrian! They started jumping, too, and we chanted, Rocky! Rocky! together for a few special moments.[1]

* * * * *

It wasn't possible to explain to my daughters how meaningful this was, but I suspected there were a few other middle-aged guys out there who would understand. These were the same guys who, like me, had once done one-handed push-ups on their living room floors and who, like me, had later been knocked around by life.

Like Rocky Balboa, I had learned that "it ain't about how hard you hit, it's about how hard you can *get* hit and keep moving forward."[2] For a moment, anyway, it was enough to feel like flying again.

---

1. http://www.youtube.com/watch?v=fhBhhwYayKg.

2. Sylvester Stallone, director, *Rocky Balboa* (Hollywood, Calif.: Metro-Goldwyn-Mayer, 2006).

# Chapter 25
# Rest

After settling in Chattanooga, Cindy and I had continued to grapple with the Seventh-day Adventist faith of our childhood. Was it true, as many of our friends were telling us, that the Sabbath commandment had been abolished by Christ? As painful as it was to question our long-held beliefs, Cindy and I were determined to follow Scripture wherever it led. In our first year in Chattanooga, we visited seventeen different churches, most of them not Adventist. We enjoyed worshiping and studying at these churches, and we learned much from them. Still, we couldn't find a convincing argument that the Sabbath of Scripture had been abolished—that Christians today were better off without it. The best I could tell, the real reason that many early Christians, most of them Gentiles, had distanced themselves from the Sabbath was because they wanted to distance themselves from the Jews. Though uncomfortable, this explanation made the most sense.

Keeping the Sabbath certainly didn't save anyone, as some Sabbatarians incorrectly taught. But resting on the Sabbath remained a powerful symbol of our salvation-rest in Christ. It helped guard against overworking and against idolatry—worshiping the work of our own hands. Six days of labor was enough, God had said. The seventh day, Sabbath, is a time for rest, rejuvenation, and worship.

* * * * *

In late 2007, the business began to turn flat again. Our newspaper carriers were taking a beating from the Internet and had to cut back on their pages. We still had some money in the bank, and I was faced with a dilemma. Should I use the remaining funds to try to grow the business again, or should I just mail a final check to Dever Designs and call it a day? Dever Designs was our final patient creditor. After the crash, they had never pressured us to pay more than we could. We trust you, Andy, they said. Use your money to get back on your feet.

At the time of the crash, we could have paid Dever Designs only about 10 percent of what we owed them. Now we could pay most of it. The right thing to do, I decided, would be to mail the check and close down *The Front Porch* for good.

In some ways, the decision wasn't that hard. I had gotten awfully tired of working alone for so many years; the weekly deadlines had taken their toll on me. Even Joe had once called to see how I was holding up personally. At the time I had just gotten shingles, which I attributed to other stress in my life. Joe encouraged me to take care of my health first. Though he appreciated what I was doing, he didn't want me to feel too much pressure to get him paid back. He said that he even felt somewhat responsible for letting us go forward in the first place. Joe's words felt like a balm to me. He'd forgiven us without even being asked.

The other reason I was ready to be done was that I just didn't have my old ambition anymore. I was tired of striving for something big. I'd come to enjoy teaching more and had recently taken a full-time position at Southern Adventist University teaching journalism. Compared to what I'd been through, spending the day with college students and the evening with family suddenly seemed wonderfully appealing. After six years of laboring on this business, I knew it was time to rest. Alone in my home office, I wrote an e-mail message to our newspaper carriers, thanking them for their business and giving notice that we were shutting down for good. I stared at the message for a while. Then I pressed send. It was all over. *The Front Porch* ended just as quietly as it began.

* * * * *

This must have been how Dad felt.

After we'd had the auction and moved to Orlando, Dad had been in a dark and bitter mood. Our first Saturday night in our apartment, Dad was frustrated that we didn't have cable television yet, so he suggested that he and I go buy a set of rabbit ears to hold us over. We'll need to stop at an ATM first, he said, as we walked to the car.

I pulled out my wallet. Here, Dad, I said. I've got some money.

No, that's OK, he mumbled. I'll stop at an ATM.

No, just take this, I said, pushing some bills at him.

He looked at me and said, I've got pride, too, you know.

I had never seen such pain in his eyes.

A few weeks later, I drove to college in Chattanooga. A few weeks after that, Dad drove to Oregon. He was trying to grow another business—selling music accompaniment tracks to Rotary International—in an attempt to quickly get back on his feet. Dad was a gifted keyboardist and was single-handedly recording background tapes for nearly all of the songs in the Rotary songbook.

Dad didn't need to drive all the way from Florida to Oregon to sell accompaniment tapes. He could have done it from our small apartment in Orlando. In reality, Dad and Mom just needed some time to themselves, so while Mom taught middle school English in Orlando, Dad worked out of a house owned by some relatives in Portland. Dad sat in that house day after day, making Rotary accompaniment tapes. Then he sat there waiting for orders to come in, waiting for the fax machine to move. A few orders came in, but not many. Not nearly enough to cover the finished sets of Rotary accompaniment tapes stacked next to Dad. The idea hadn't worked. There wasn't going to be a quick way out of the mud.

For Christmas, we all flew out to Oregon to see Dad—our tickets apparently paid by someone else. First, we drove over to the house where Dad was staying. Then Angel and I were brought over to our cousins' place while Mom and Dad stayed back at the house. They needed to talk for a while. Christmas that year was different from usual. Our aunts, uncles, and cousins had been helping to support migrant workers living in sheds nearby. These workers, said Aunt Lorrie, were Mexicans who'd found their way to Oregon to pick fruit. They were really struggling, so rather than exchange gifts with each other, we were all going to take gifts to the migrant worker families. We piled in the cars and drove over to see the migrant workers and their families living in long rows of unheated sheds. It was cold in the sheds, but the families were bundled warm and smiling big as they saw us entering with gifts. The children sat wide-eyed in their parents' arms. We handed out our gifts, wishing we'd had more. As we drove away, we were all aglow with how good it felt to help these families. Later that week, we went again.

For years, Mom would mention what a deep impact the visit to the migrant workers had had on Dad. It seemed to bring out the better parts of Dad—the natural generosity and sensitivity that were part of who he was. Every Christmas when we'd lived in Minnesota, Dad would drive to Pamida and load up shopping carts with presents for poor families in our church. Then, undercover as Santa, Dad would distribute the presents at our annual church Christmas party. It was at these times that I felt most proud of him.

After Christmas in Oregon, Mom, Angel, and I flew back to Florida. Then a few weeks later—in time for my spring break from college—Dad came home too. He drove straight through from Portland to Orlando in his worn-out Datsun 280ZX Turbo, the car he'd bought years earlier at the height of his success.

As it turned out, Rotary music wasn't the only music Dad made in Oregon. As my spring break ended and I was loading up my car, Dad walked outside. He pulled a cassette tape from his pocket. Handing me the tape, he said, Here's just something to listen to if you get bored.

OK, I said.

This goodbye was different from all our previous goodbyes. Normally as I was leaving, Dad would slip me some spending money—maybe a hundred dollars, sometimes more. Giving was how Dad expressed his love to us. But this time, Dad didn't have any money to give. So he gave what the humble and the children give—a gift he had made himself.

As I left the apartment complex, I slipped in the cassette. A single song filled the car for the next ten minutes. At some point out in Oregon, after the visit to the migrant workers, Dad had recorded the song "I Am Willing, Lord." Dad used to play this song when I was a kid, but I'd never heard him play it quite like this.

The opening verse began with simple keyboard:

Sometimes when I am down
And I don't feel like you're around, Oh Lord.
Feeling so sorry for me.

Not knowing that all the while you're working to see.
If when I'm put through the fire,
I'll come out shining like gold.
Oh, Lord, please don't ever stop working with me
Till you see I can be all you want me to be.

As the song progressed to the chorus, Dad had added additional tracks and flourishes: a bed of strings, a horn section, a booming bass.

I am willing, Lord. I am willing, Lord.
To be just exactly what you want me to be.[1]

By the song's final lines, Dad had pulled out all the stops: a full string section, shooting stars, voices singing *Aah.* It was as though Dad had poured absolutely everything he had into this one meaningful song. I was positive that tears had been streaming down his face. I rewound the song several times on my drive to Tennessee, thinking about the difference I was seeing in Dad. As he had handed me the cassette tape, his anger and pride seemed to be gone. At some point, he had made the decision to rest.

Shortly after Dad returned home, he and Mom received an unexpected invitation from a pastor friend to play the keyboard and piano for a new worship service at church. It would be a big deal—a weekly commitment with music practice every Friday evening. Dad and Mom accepted the invitation. For years to come, they would play music together, mentoring other young musicians as well. Instead of a wincing under a migraine every Friday evening, Dad was worshiping the Lord.

1. "I Am Willing, Lord," music and lyrics by Kurt Kaiser.

## *Chapter 26*

# Renewal

I was amazed at how much freedom I felt after closing down the business. I was still plenty busy with teaching and freelance-editing work, but none of these had the grip on me that the business had. I wasn't mentally and emotionally consumed by these things. I wasn't going to sleep and waking up thinking about them. I knew that the problem with *The Front Porch* hadn't been the product itself—it was a good product. Nor had there been anything wrong with pursuing a professional dream.

The problem was how much I had stretched and strained to make the dream happen. By choosing to take such a big gamble in this business, I had, by default, drawn myself down in other areas of life. I had lost a sense of space and balance in my life. Risking everything for a dream had once sounded so heroic, so desirable—until I'd realized what the "everything" was. By tethering my own happiness to the ups and downs of the business, I had little left emotionally for what mattered most to me: my faith and family. I wanted them back, in fullness.

*****

A friend of mine, Gary, had once told me about something he did every January—he would read through the entire Bible in a single month. I was astounded by this. But to my surprise, it would mean reading only about forty pages a day. This wouldn't allow for deep, careful study, but Gary said to read the Bible like any other book was a rewarding experience. I resolved to try it.

Day after day, through January 2008, I devoted myself to intensive Scripture reading. I read in the morning, between classes, at lunch, and after the girls had gone to bed. I couldn't believe how swiftly I was moving through it. In just a few days, I was already through the books of Moses and on to Joshua. More important than how much I was reading was the *way* I was reading. For the first time in years, I wasn't reading Scripture through the lens of my own ambitions. I was letting the text speak for itself. I was delighting myself in the Lord.

The readings stayed on my mind all day long. Because I didn't have time for anything else—TV, the Internet, sports, news—my mind was stuffed with Scripture. As I read through the Old Testament, I felt all the emotions of the Hebrew people's up-and-down relationship with God: how they drifted away from God when things were going well and then crawled back to Him when things weren't. It was a cycle repeated over and over. By the time I reached the New Testament, I felt the deep longing for the Messiah who would save us all, in spite of ourselves.

In my intensive read-through, I starred verses and whole books that made a particular impact on me: Deuteronomy, Ezra, and Isaiah in the Old Testament, and Matthew, Hebrews, and James in the New Testament. The book that spoke the most powerfully to me was the New Testament book of Ephesians. Written by Paul, Ephesians was an especially strong call to take the Christian walk seriously. I found the middle section of the letter particularly compelling, in which Paul calls his readers to "walk in a manner worthy of the calling to which you have been called" (Ephesians 4:1, ESV). It wasn't enough, Paul said, just to be saved; we were also called to make the most of our time (see Ephesians 5:16). Lately I hadn't been doing that. It had been several years since I had been actively involved in church. I was merely dragging along.

The past Christmas I'd gotten my saxophone out to play a solo called "Immanuel" at the church we were attending. Just before I started playing, the band leader introduced me to the congregation as "Cindy Nash's husband." I laughed to myself. My identity at church had become Cindy's husband. Given my lack of involvement, it was a completely appropriate introduction.

But now, as I devoted myself to Scripture reading, I began to wonder about making a contribution to my faith again. Maybe we could get a few families together and study Ephesians and do some service projects together with our kids. Just something simple and informal.

* * * * *

During this same period, I began to think about another spiritual opportunity. Ever since I was a boy, I had been enamored of the Holy Land. Mom would read Bible stories to Angel and me at night, and I'd sit there, thinking how cool it would be to visit places like Jerusalem and the Sea of Galilee for myself.

If I could go any place in the world, I asked Mom, do you know where I'd like to go?

Where? she said crisply, with a knowing smile.

The Holy Land!

Wow! she said. The Holy Land? That sounds like a *great* trip to take!

But at the age of thirty-seven, I still hadn't taken it.

Though I didn't make much money as a college teacher, I did have one really nice perk: a professional allowance of about twenty-seven hundred dollars a year. When I put in a request to travel to Israel and do some writing, the request was granted. I wanted Cindy to come along, but she begged off. She didn't want us both being *that* far away from the girls. Also, she had visited Israel before. Instead, we decided that I could take Ally along. I had enough frequent flyer miles on United Airlines for her ticket to be free.

Now at the age of ten, Ally was thrilled when we told her about the trip. In fact, she began to talk about the Holy Land all the time. As she did, I began to wonder how Morgan was feeling. She was only eight—I wasn't sure she'd even want to take a trip like this.

Morgan, I asked one evening, do you feel bad that you're not going to the Holy Land with Ally and me?

Well, she said slowly, I did have a good long cry about it.

I phoned United. I was taking them both. This ought to be interesting.

# *Chapter 27*
# Lake Home

With just two weeks until the Holy Land trip, we thought we'd just stay home for Memorial Day weekend—maybe go for a swim at the community pool. But on the morning of Memorial Day, Cindy got an invitation from one of her hospital coworkers, Lynn, inviting us out to her lake home for a day of jet skiing. Yes! Jet skiing sounded great. We couldn't change into our swimming suits quickly enough.

We spent the day jet skiing and swimming, and for supper we relaxed on Lynn's back deck, devouring hamburgers and hot dogs. I was surprised that Lynn hadn't had holiday plans; she was a smart, attractive woman in her early fifties. As I looked out across Lynn's huge level yard leading to the water's edge, I was reminded of my childhood lake home back in Minnesota—for which I still felt an occasional twinge of longing.

Even after eighteen years, Lake Melissa still left an indelible impression on me. I remembered how it felt to stand on the south shore, watching the blue herons fly from right to left across the beautiful Minnesota sky. I spent many days on the south shore, cleaning beaches at our own cottage and at Orlo's resort cottages next door. Through the years, whenever I'd needed to remember which direction was which, I always returned mentally to Lake Melissa and pictured myself on the south shore: west was left, north was straight, east was right. Lake Melissa was still my guiding star.

When I was in college, my own English teacher had asked us to write about our favorite place in the world. Late that evening in my dorm room, I turned on my computer and, in a single painful burst, wrote about Lake Melissa.

> . . . The lake itself is deep in the middle, great for bass fishing, but shallow and mushy around the edges. (The church joins us for wiffleball Saturday night and, when we all get hot and jump in the water, everyone remarks how mushy and gooey the bottom of our lake is, and I wonder what they want us to do about it.) When it has not rained much and the lake is low, we push our boat out past the muck because we do not want to bend the stainless steel prop, which cost a lot, you know. It already has a few nicks on it. Anytime there is glassy water on an evening my dad is home, I ski. Angel and her friend Nicole tube. And the boat paces back and forth in front of our A-frame cabin on Lake Melissa until Mom comes out onto the cedar porch and rings the big brass bell, which means it is time to eat.
>
> Back inside our cottage, we take turns pouring the white dressing on our salads while Casey, our West Highland White Terrier, and Gypsy, Angel's pet raccoon, chase each other around the bar stools. The evening is cool and quiet, and Orlo drops by "to see how you folks are doing" and tell me to clean the beaches in the morning because he will be in town. I decide how late I can get up and still be done by the time he gets back as I turn on the television. "Not that stupid show again," says Angel, referring to the "Great KX Hole-in-One Show," my favorite. And as Casey scratches the door to go out and my parents talk about taking the Jeep over to the Flea Market Sunday with Burgesons, I am content with our life on the lake, never dreaming that a financial crisis will force an auction next summer where we will have to sell our favorite place in the world, piece by piece, at an opening bid of five dollars.

There were times when I still wondered whether we'd ever be able to live on the water.

As we finished eating, Lynn told us why she had invited us over. She didn't have anyone to spend Memorial Day with. Lynn had recently separated, her kids were grown, and she hadn't seen her own parents much over the years. Her father had always been a busy and wealthy man. Each January he would send Lynn a large check to cover gifts for her kids that year. But Lynn didn't want her dad's money. All I ever wanted, she said, was his time and attention.

Lynn said that for her fiftieth birthday she got a wonderful surprise. Her dad joined her for a cross-country bike ride. Through misty eyes, she said it was one of the highlights of her life. As Lynn spoke, a deep awakening washed over me. Here we were, sitting at this gorgeous lake home, and none of it really mattered to this woman. None of it really mattered if she didn't have people to share it with.

Like scales falling from my eyes, I realized why our lake home had been so special to me as a boy. It wasn't because of the lake or the cottage, as nice as they were. It was because my family was there. Dad and Mom and Angel—*it was because they were there.* How could I have been so shortsighted? It wasn't the *place* that was special. It was the *people.*

I thought about other places we had lived—more modest places, including our first Florida apartment at the Verandahs. I had great memories with my family there too. In fact, years later when I had returned to Florida and walked through the apartment complex, the emotions that I felt there were eerily similar to the emotions I felt when I'd returned to visit Lake Melissa. Sure, the lake had the soft spin of the boat lift as Dad lowered the speedboat into the water, but the apartment complex had Dad humorously adjusting his red, white, and blue headband as he prepared for a big serve. Both places had Mom's laugh and Angel's loony escapades. Both places were haunted by my family.

I thought about visits to my relatives on both sides. My dad's parents lived in a regal house with a pool; my mom's parents and brother lived in a small house with simple furniture. Which place had I loved more? I couldn't decide because I couldn't decide which *people* loved me more. My happiness wasn't about the place; it was about the people. As Lynn spoke, I felt a tremendous sense of relief, a burden lifted. My kids didn't need everything I'd had to be as happy as I was. All they needed was me.

Later I e-mailed Dad and told him about this—how I'd come to realize that my kids will love their memories with me no matter where we are and what we have. Dad replied later that day. "Bingo!" he wrote. "It took me longer than it has taken you to realize that. Congratulations!"

## *Chapter 28*

# Holy Land

Israel was everything I'd hoped for—and in one unexpected way, much more.

After the night flight, the girls and I spent a full day resting and body-surfing in the Mediterranean Sea, in full view of Joppa—where Jonah had famously tried to sail out of God's reach. Between waves, I teased the girls about spotting large fish.

No, I'm serious—I really do see one this time.

Dadd*eee*!

The next day we went up to Jerusalem, like so many before us. As we stepped from the taxi into history, I'd never seen the girls' eyes more wide open. Hand in tight hand, the three of us wove through crowded markets—Jewish, Muslim, Christian—to the serene, beautiful, but improbable Garden tomb. Late the same evening, we still had time to see where Jesus had more likely been buried. Some people don't want the Church of the Holy Sepulchre to be *the place* because they don't like its aesthetics; it's too dark, too confusing, and too crowded. But strangely, just before closing, we were almost the only ones there.

The dark corridors of the massive church did confuse us, and after several left turns in a row, we just stood still, utterly lost. In front of us was some type of shrine with candles at the entrance. Another traveler was passing by.

Excuse me, I said. What is that over there?

That, he said slowly, is the sepulcher of Christ.

I was stunned. We were here, at the tomb? Alone?

I led the girls into the outer chamber where a young nun knelt in fervent prayer, like an angel of the Lord beckoning us forward. We passed by her and ducked into the inner chamber, where more candles illumined a large flat rock on the right side of the tomb, just as the Gospels described it. The girls said nothing and looked a little awestruck as we huddled there together, touching the smooth rock. Somehow I knew that this was the place.

*****

In the days that followed, we visited all the sites I had so carefully chosen in my travel guides. At one point, as we were walking past the court of Caiaphas—where Peter had denied that he knew Jesus—we struck up a conversation with another father and child. The father's name, ironically, was Peter Nash. He was an American Jew, traveling with his son to Israel for the first time. Back home he taught college English. We certainly had a lot in common.

Later that evening, we joined thousands of Jews at the Western Wall to welcome *Shabbat.* Over the years, even within my Sabbatarian faith community, I hadn't exactly noticed an eagerness to be associated with Jews any more than necessary. My maternal grandmother's maiden name was Israel; her father's name was John Moses Israel. Surely my sweet little grandma had *some* Jewish blood in her. Yet, as my uncle Paul once told me laughingly, Grandma rarely talked about her father's Jewish heritage. She preferred to emphasize her mom's *Danish* heritage. I'd heard my friends describe similar attitudes in their own older relatives: a subtle distancing from anything Jewish.

But that's not how I felt at all. As we stood near the wall, watching the dancing circles of Jewish girls and boys, I couldn't have felt more privileged to have Jewish blood in me—and more proud to share their Sabbath. With all its problems, my faith community was the definition of Judeo-Christian; I'd never felt more happy to be part of it.

The Western Wall, the Holy Sepulchre, the upper room—as a Judeo-Christian I knew these places would remain with me, enhancing my reading of Scripture. Still, as much as I treasured what we were seeing and experiencing, the sites themselves wouldn't become the story of the trip for me. Instead, it would be the two people that I shared them with—my daughters.

Thursday in Jerusalem had been one of the circled days of our trip. Thursday was the last day of the week that non-Muslims were allowed to visit the temple mount. We were leaving Sunday for the Dead Sea region and then up to Galilee, so Thursday was our only chance to visit the place where the most orthodox still fear to tread; they don't want to risk walking where the Holy of Holies might have been.

I had heard how beautiful it was to approach the temple mount from the east in the morning light, hiking down from the Mount of Olives and Gethsemane, so that was our big plan for the day. But our plans took an unexpected turn. Morgan threw up several times the night before. By morning she said that she felt a little better and that she wanted to see the temple mount. I quickly deemed her fit enough, and we slipped into the required long pants and skirts, respectively.

We took a taxi to the Lion's Gate and entered on foot. Immediately to our left, I saw a temple mount entrance. As we approached security guards, someone called out, Are you Muslim? When I said No, they motioned to continue on the road we were already on. Keep walking up the Via Dolorosa, they said, and then take the next left.

The road was narrow, cobbled, and uphill, and Morgan began to tug on my hand. Morgan didn't usually let me carry her anymore. Like all twinkle-eyed daughters, she had grown beyond her dad's arms. But she kept tugging.

Sweetheart, I asked, do you want me to carry you?

She nodded and lifted her arms. She was my little girl again.

Resting her hand on my neck, Morgan sipped from her water bottle as we trudged along together. In time we turned left and found the entrance meant for us, near the Western Wall. We spent two special hours on the temple mount. By the end, Morgan was rejuvenated and her old self. She poured her bottled water over Ally's head.

It wasn't until later that afternoon, as I watched the girls giggle away a hot day with a cool swim, that it dawned on me. The street on which I'd carried Morgan was the Via Dolorosa, the way of the cross. Intellectually I had known this, but I wasn't thinking of it at the time. I wasn't thinking about the place—what it looked like, smelled like, felt like under my feet. I was thinking only about my daughter. As she had leaned softly against me, my sole desire at that moment was simply to hold her, to ease her burden—the strange yet welcome love that, probably more than anything else, lets a sinful parent know the heart of the Father. Somehow carrying her had felt lighter than not carrying her. It helped me to understand.

*****

This would become the unexpected story for me: the dependence of my daughters on me. It wasn't just physical dependence; it was total emotional trust. Each morning my sleepy-eyed girls blinked open the day with the words, Where are we going today, Daddy?

This question amazed me. Here we were, six thousand miles from home, and they slept peacefully at night for one reason: they were with me. I was humbled by their trusting spirits, and in this place, the lesson was most appropriate. When the Hebrew people had turned from their own wisdom and relied instead on the Lord—had rested in Him—they were most at peace.

*Where are we going today, Daddy?* The words hit me hardest as we drove through the volatile West Bank to the Dead Sea. The Hertz rental agent had assured me that this wasn't an unusual route for either Jew or foreigner. Still, our own government had advised against travel through the West Bank; my travel guide didn't even review Bethlehem, Bethany, and Jericho, all located here. Yet here we were—first time visitors driving alone through the forbidden land. That night at our kibbutz, I lay in tears, heavy with the unyielding burden of caring for my girls—deeply touched by their confidence in me.

The next afternoon we left the desert region for the lushness of Galilee. There was another place I wanted to see.

# Chapter 29
# Tabgha

I needed to come here.

I'm at the lake on a calm spring morning. I'm up to my knees in the water, and some of the rocks hurt my feet, but I absolutely don't mind because this is about the happiest I've felt in my life.

* * * * *

I'm here at Tabgha—on the northwestern shore of the freshwater lake called the Sea of Galilee. I've thought about this place for such a long time, and to actually be here feels like a dream.

When we pulled in this morning, it was beautifully quiet. Exiting our car, the girls and I took the short trail leading past a small chapel and a sculpture of Peter and Jesus. The statue arrested my attention. Peter kneels before Jesus, his head thrown back, his left hand reaching out. Jesus stands above the penitent disciple, his right arm extended in blessing. In his left arm, Jesus holds out a shepherd's rod. Peter grasps it with his right hand. The right side is the side of faith.

We walked past the statue down to the shore where Jesus had prepared a breakfast of bread and fish for the disciples on a "fire of coals." The phrase "fire of coals" in John 21:9 (NKJV) is found in just one other place in all of Scripture—in John 18:18, where Peter stands at a "fire of coals" and denies that he is one of Jesus' disciples.

I had figured that we'd just stand on the shore for a while and look out into the lake. But down the shoreline, I saw two men from Asia walking out into the water, as though they wanted to get as close as possible to that long-ago fishing boat. Here we were—Christian men from worlds away, converging at Tabgha. The news of the Nazarene had reached both of our lands. Rolling up my pants, I walked out into the water with the other disciples.

*****

Now, as I balance myself on the rocks in the cool water, it occurs to me that I'm here in the springtime, just as Peter was when he returned to Galilee after the Resurrection. The water temperature probably would have been about the same, and when Peter piled out of his fishing boat to get to the Lord, he may have walked across these same rocks.

What doesn't occur to me until later is that many of the deep emotions I feel on this morning were also felt, undoubtedly in a much greater sense, by Peter. Like me, he had experienced his own broken dream—his plans hadn't worked out like he thought they would. Like me, he had reluctantly developed a certain look in his eye: a look of serenity, of submission, of finally releasing what he had held on to so fiercely. Like me, he probably didn't understand this look in others until he saw it in himself. He didn't know humiliation until he was knocked flat and forced to acknowledge defeat.

I'm struck by the poetry of Peter's experience—including the strange reappearance of the number three in his life. Peter was the third disciple called by Jesus, he denied Jesus three times and, in their third meeting after the Resurrection, he was reinstated with the threefold question, "Do you love Me?" Later on, in Joppa, when Peter was called by this same Jesus to take the gospel to the Gentiles, a sheet full of unclean animals was lowered, and Peter was given a threefold instruction: "Get up, Peter. Kill and eat" (Acts 10:13). Immediately, three guests appeared at the door. Whether this is mere coincidence or not, the strange symmetry of the experience is at least interesting.

I feel the same when I later notice a strange symmetry to my own experience. But for me the number is not three but seven, a number deeply imbedded into me since childhood. As I'd learned, *Tabgha* means "seven springs," and as it happens, I'm here seven years and seven months after my life-altering experience began. It has taken me that long to learn how to let go. I don't know whether to view all this as anything more than the poetry of life. But it's poetry I enjoy.

So is this: I happen to be here at the age of thirty-seven, which brings both numbers together—Peter's and mine. Making things all the more memorable was my strange new acquaintance in Jerusalem with Peter Nash, the American Jew who, like me, was traveling to Israel for the first time and who, like me, was a college writing professor. The place where we struck up our conversation happened to be the path leading past the high priest's courtyard, where Peter had denied knowing Jesus.

I don't know quite what to think about this. Years earlier I'd heard my friend Clifford Goldstein tell about his first visit to Israel. Cliff had grown up in Miami Beach, and on his journey to Israel, he had met another young Jewish man named Clifford Goldstein who *also* had grown up in Miami Beach, who, only months apart, had *also* stayed at the same kibbutz in Israel—in fact, who stayed in the same room and placed the same books on the same bookshelf, who, like Cliff, had a blond Danish girlfriend named Tine (but not the same Tine) while on the kibbutz, and who, like Cliff, was a writer.

You asked God for a sign, someone told Cliff. What more do you want? The Lord is calling you by name. Shortly thereafter, Cliff became a believer in another young Jewish Man.

What is it about this place? Do these types of coincidences mean anything? I really don't know. But I know that in Scripture, at least, the Lord seems to care about the details of our lives, right down to our names. He changed the name of Abram to Abraham, Jacob to Israel, Simon to Peter. Maybe He still calls us by name and number at certain points in our lives.

More important to me than these symbols is the experience itself. I feel so happy here, so light and at peace. For once, I feel as though I don't have to strive for anything. I don't have to give; I have only to receive—just as in the distance Peter received the blessing of Christ. It begins to dawn on me: Tabgha is the place where you reach the end of yourself, where you let go of your own plans and humbly bow before God's. This was certainly the case for Peter, and ironically, given where all this started, it has become that for me as well. More than a physical place, however, Tabgha is a spiritual place to which all disciples must, at some point, pay a visit—a place where they must answer the questions of Christ.

*****

I think more about the question Jesus asked Peter on this very shore, "Do you truly love me more than these?" (John 21:15). I've had an increasingly strong sense about what Jesus meant. I don't think Jesus was asking, "Do you love Me more than the other disciples do?" It's true that Peter had once compared himself to the other disciples, saying, "Even if all fall away on account of you, I never will. . . . Even if I have to die with you, I will never disown you" (Matthew 26:33, 35). But there are difficulties with this interpretation.

First, when Peter said he would never disown Jesus, all the other disciples said the same thing. It wasn't just Peter. The competitiveness among the disciples was well established. More than once they had gotten into an argument about who was the greatest. The brothers James and John seemed particularly competitive. They once asked Jesus if they could sit at His right and left when He established His kingdom. Jesus replied, "You don't know what you are asking. . . . Can you drink the cup I drink or be baptized with the baptism I am baptized with?" (Mark 10:38). They confidently replied that they could. When the other disciples heard about this, they were livid with James and John. The problem with competitiveness wasn't unique to Peter.

Another clue about what Jesus meant by His question, "Do you truly love me more than these?" is Peter's response to it. Peter answers, "Yes." It seems unlikely, at this point, that Peter would answer, "Yes" if Jesus were asking, "Do you love Me more than the other disciples do?" This may have been Peter's confident mind-set before the Crucifixion, but it wasn't now. No longer was Peter going to put his affection for Jesus up against that of others. Saying, "Yes, Lord, I love You more than the other disciples love You," would have indicated a continued problem, not a solution. If Jesus were indeed asking, "Do you love Me more than the other disciples do?" Peter would not have answered "Yes."

Instead, I've come to believe that Jesus was asking a much deeper question: "Simon, son of John, do you love Me more than you love these fish?" The strongest evidence for this comes from the text itself. Just before Jesus says, "Do you truly love me more than these?" He says, "Bring some of the *fish* you have just caught" (John 21:10; emphasis added). Why hadn't I seen this earlier? As an English teacher, I should have noticed it. The word *these* is a plural noun, and the nearest corresponding plural noun is *fish.* When Jesus said "these," He was likely referring to the large fish that He'd just asked the disciples to bring to Him. Jesus didn't need the fish for breakfast. He had already prepared bread and fish on the burning coals. It was for another reason that He told the disciples to bring the fish. He wanted to ask Peter about them. Contextually, given the location and Peter's background, this makes perfect sense.

By the time Jesus met Peter at Galilee, Peter had had time to reconsider his identity as a fisherman disciple. He had come to realize that what was most holding him back from full discipleship was his own will. His ambition for power, and perhaps, wealth in the kingdom of God was really no different from the ambitions that he had brought to his former life of fishing. That's why Jesus wanted to meet Peter here on the same Galilee shore where He had first called him. Here, on Peter's home surf, Jesus wanted to give him a chance to demonstrate his growth. And what better way than to give to the self-declared former disciple what had once been his dream—a net teeming with large fish? Jesus wanted to ask Peter about fish and everything they represented.

In doing so, Jesus reverts to Peter's old identity, Simon, son of John. With these words Jesus had first called Simon to ministry. And now He calls him again.

"Simon son of John," Jesus says, "do you truly love me more than these?"

"Yes, Lord," he says, "you know that I love you" (verse 15).

The disciple was back and more full of faith than ever. The last time he'd seen Jesus exercise authority over fish, he had cowered in the boat and said, "Go away from me, Lord" (Luke 5:8). But on this morning, he had hurled himself out of the boat and scrambled *toward* Jesus on the shore. He no longer cared much about the fish. He cared only about Jesus. Simon finally got it. And he departed the shore as Peter.

## *Chapter 30*
# Emanuel

When we'd first decided to travel to Israel, I was sitting in bed with Cindy one evening. You know, I said, the Jordan River would be a neat place for the girls to be baptized.

I felt Cindy's body stiffen. Sor-ry! she replied forcefully.

I had figured as much. There was no way she was going to miss the baptism of her daughters. After a few quiet moments, however, I heard Cindy sigh. Oh, she said, it *would* be so special for them.

* * * * *

Ally, Morgan, and I walk back up the path to our car. We were departing the Sea of Galilee, but only in a sense. This same water is headed for the same destination we are—the Jordan River. As we drive south along the shore, the girls are more quiet than usual. To be mere minutes from not only their own baptism but *their baptism in the Jordan River*—well, this was somber stuff. The moment has taken their breath away.

We pull into the parking lot, which is, for the moment, remarkably free of tour buses. Good—we've picked the right time of day. To get to the riverbank itself, we have to walk through a building where a young Jewish-Christian woman meets us.

Hi, I say, we're here for the girls' baptism.

Very good, she says. You can rent their robes at the counter.

Oh, it's OK, I tell her. They brought an extra change of clothes.

Oh, I'm sorry, she says in her best English, but it's, um—it's impossible to be baptized without renting a robe.

I sigh inwardly. I know I shouldn't say it. And even as I do, I'm sure that she's heard it hundreds of times before.

Did Jesus need a robe to be baptized?

She smiles knowingly. I'm sorry, sir.

I appreciate her gracious reply and let the matter rest. We rent the robes at the counter, and, the truth is, they look great on the girls: flowing and white. As they emerge from the changing room, they've got big smiles on their faces. Oh, sweet daughters. What did I do to deserve the joy you bring to me?

A wooden walkway runs adjacent to the Jordan, with several ramps about twenty yards apart, leading down to the water. *Every single ramp is empty. We have the place to ourselves. Perfect.*

It isn't conventional to baptize when you're not a pastor; this is a convention I'm choosing to ignore. I hadn't found any biblical reason for a Christian parent not to baptize his or her children. In fact, the more I'd thought about it, the more biblical it seemed. For the past few months, Cindy and I had been studying and praying with the girls to prepare them for this day.

Daddy, let's go here, Ally says, pointing to a spot she likes. We follow the handrails down the ramp, back and forth, back and forth.

We get Morgan set up on the video camera. Then Ally and I walk hand in hand down into the cool waters of the Jordan. The sun shines down.

Baptism, we had taught the girls, represents a dying to self—a symbolic laying of ourselves in a watery grave. In a way, it hardly seems right for the girls to "die to self" when they're still so young and innocent.

*So young and innocent—like lambs without spot or blemish.* When I think about it like this, it does seem right. How much better to give yourself to Christ in youth and innocence—rather than in decay and guilt.

I baptize my girls in the Jordan River. It's only the three of us, but our faith teaches us that we're not alone.

* * * * *

Later that evening, our last in Israel, I phone Cindy.

Well, the girls had a beautiful baptism today.

*Ohhh,* she says softly, her voice trembling. The moment is bittersweet.

We feel the same. No matter how special Israel has been, the trip hasn't felt complete without Cindy and Summer. Two pieces of our hearts are still back home.

The next morning, we throw most of our luggage in the trunk but keep one package up front with us. A few days earlier in Jerusalem, we had spotted something that dazzled us: a wooden Passover fountain with colorful hand-painted scenes of Jerusalem. A large wooden cup sat atop the fountain, and when you filled it with grape juice and then poured, the juice flowed out of eight chutes into eight small wooden cups.

Oh, Daddy, please! the girls had begged. Mommy will just love it!

I agreed. The fountain wasn't cheap, but it really was special. It was made by a company called Emanuel, the Hebrew word meaning "God with us."

We had carried the fountain with us from Jerusalem to Galilee, and now we carry it from Galilee to the airport. Twenty hours later, we carry it into our house and watch Cindy and Summer unwrap it together.

E-man-uel, Cindy says slowly as she opens the box. Hanging all over her, the girls quickly explain that it's a Passover fountain—you pour grape juice in the top and it comes out into these little cups. We can all have Communion *together,* Mommy, all of us here right at home.

And once more we're complete.

## *Chapter 31*

# Reprint

The morning after our trip, I wake up at 3:30 A.M. and wander downstairs. A few minutes later, so do Ally and Morgan. We're jet-lagged. As the three of us sit together in the dark, I realize that these are the remnant moments from our trip. We're still getting Israel out of our systems. In a sense, though, I don't *want* to get Israel out of my system. On our trip I had loved how focused I was—not only on the Holy Land itself but on the other holy parts of my life: my faith and my family.

I've been on inspiring trips before; I know that this feeling will fade. It will go away unless I fight to keep it. In the days that follow, I make a few decisions. I decide to cut back on some of the clutter in my life—the television and Internet that can so easily crowd my day. They weren't present on our trip, and I knew we were better for it. I also begin to look hard at our family budget—how we're always tight month to month. Two years earlier, we decided to buy a nice home in the country so that we could have pygmy goats and plenty of space. The only problem was, we had very little space left financially and emotionally. It isn't easy—not at all—to reconsider life patterns, to take a hard look at personal weaknesses and hereditary tendencies. But, as I'm coming to realize, the way of Christ isn't meant to be easy. By losing our life, He said, we will gain it. Patiently, He waits for that to happen.

*****

On the last day of summer, Cindy and I take the girls to our community pool. We've been coming here a lot lately, getting our fill of swimming before the fall breezes blow.

On this day, we invite our friends to swim with us: Alex and Nicole and their little girl, Audrey. Alex and I went to college together, and then he became a pastor in Atlanta. The past year he moved to Chattanooga to work at the large church near the college campus where I teach journalism. The church has four worship services—three in the main sanctuary and a contemporary-style service called Connect in an auditorium down the road.

All of us jump in the pool with the girls, and between games of Marco Polo and splash-the-other-person's-face, Alex mentions a comment that one of his pastor colleagues, Wolf, had made earlier that week. Wolf was wondering whether I might have any interest in being part-time pastor of Connect.

What?

Yeah, Alex says. He was just wondering.

I'm taken aback. I really don't know Wolf at all. A few days earlier, I'd seen him at a Chinese takeout, but that was about it. We hadn't ever talked. I'm a journalist; why would he think of me?

The girls want us to flip them backward into the water. Between splashes I turn over Wolf's words in my mind. For the past several months, I've been feeling a renewed desire to be involved again at church. While we're toweling off, I tell Alex that I'm not sure how it could even work out, but if Wolf wanted to talk, I would do that. Maybe it could be something that Cindy and I could help with together in some capacity.

Cindy gives me a look. There's just no way.

*****

A few nights later, Cindy and I sit talking in bed. The pastors had asked us to come talk with them.

We could just explore it and see, I say.

No.

You're naturally gifted for ministry.

Andy, please—

You've led women's Bible study groups.

Yes, but that was just small scale.

Cindy, don't you have any desire for something like this at all?

She pauses. Her demeanor completely changes, and she admits a prayer that she has prayed for years: that someday she and I would have the opportunity to work in ministry together.

* * * * *

The meeting is led by John Nixon, the senior pastor. For the first few minutes, Pastor Nixon shares some background on the church, and then he invites us to share our own story. I talk about my own faith journey and about what I value in a church—a place that's committed, multigenerational, and centered on Scripture. This last point, I say, is particularly important to me. I've come to know the rewards of deep inductive study. What I would do to start, I tell them, is study the book of Ephesians together as a church.

Cindy doesn't say much until the end of the meeting. Visibly nervous, she speaks slowly. She says she isn't seeking this—not at all. But if we were asked to do it, she would view it as a calling. I feel a sense of peace settle over us. Cindy's inhibitions are beginning to thaw. The staff thanks us for coming and says they'll be in touch.

Over the next few days, I have trouble getting this church out of my mind. What surprises me is that I feel more excited about *this* than I do about publishing. This is really, really strange. For the first time in my adult life, I feel a diminishing desire for journalism. The previous summer I'd spent a week in New York helping *Reader's Digest* develop a new magazine. I was grateful for the experience and was apparently being considered to be the magazine's editor. But strangely, over the past few months, my love for publication work has faded. I actually feel more interested in leading this small worship service than I do in being editor of this big new magazine. *How weird.* If at this moment I were asked to move to New York City, I'm just not sure that I would. My heart isn't there anymore.

But what I don't want to do is to impose my own will here. For once I just want to trust the process—trust the wisdom of these Christian men and women and trust Christ. This is the spiritual realm—holy ground—and I don't want to push my plans and risk another difficult experience. I don't want to chase the wind anymore. Years ago I heard people use the term *a call* when they talked about taking a job in ministry. They wouldn't apply *for* the job. They would be called *to* the job. These days I don't hear that term as much anymore. Even in ministry, people tend to go after the job they want. In general, I see no problem with that. But in this case, I don't want to do that. I just want to wait and rest rather than go after what might be the wrong situation.

Sure enough, in the days that follow, the indications don't look good. I begin to hear about some tension between the church staff and the Connect leadership team. When their former pastor had departed, the leadership team thought that they were getting a new full-time pastor. Now they were hearing something about me and Cindy being brought on board part time. Nothing against us, but this wasn't what they had expected.

By the week's end, I feel a mixture of emotions. On one hand, I feel relieved that these dynamics have surfaced before we'd taken the job. At least we could pull back quietly. No harm, no foul. But I feel disappointed, and a little hurt. Again.

* * * * *

The next day, Sabbath, we're on our way to church. We decide to attend Connect anyway; maybe we can just get involved as new members. I swing by my office at the college to get something. My phone is blinking with a message from the day before.

I hit play and hear a voice that I haven't heard in seventeen years. The voice belongs to Debi Eldridge—a girl I'd gone to high school and college with. We'd been friends but not particularly close friends. I had no idea where Debi even lived. Why would she be calling me?

"Hey, Andy," she says, "this is a blast from the past. This is Debi Eldridge Amick calling, and I really was just calling because I felt that God asked me to. I was praying this morning, and your name came to my mind a couple of times. So I was just giving you a call . . . at the direction of God, which I know seems really strange since we haven't talked in forever. As I was praying this morning, your name came to mind, so I was praying over you—that you would walk in the fullness of God's blessings. So maybe that means something to you. Hope you and Cindy are doing great."

The message ends, and I sit at my desk for a moment. How strange to hear from Debi Eldridge. She'd left her number, but Cindy and the girls are waiting in the car.

I call Debi back Monday morning.

Debi, this is Andy.

Andy, she says, laughing. Were you surprised to hear from me?

Yeah, a little.

I ask Debi about her family and what she's doing now. She says that she and Ron have two kids, and that she's now a real estate agent in southern Georgia. We talk about old times and shared friends.

After a few minutes, she says, Hey, Andy, it's great talking to you again, but I just really want you to know that I wasn't calling to reconnect or anything. I just felt like I wasn't able to go to work Friday morning until I called you. I was praying, and I felt like God was telling me to call and give you that message—that you would walk in the fullness of God's blessings.

Thanks, Debi, I say. That was definitely unexpected, but I really appreciate it.

We say goodbye, and I return to my work.

* * * * *

Over the next few days, I feel more and more cautious about getting involved in this ministry position. I don't want to force anything and risk confusion and hurt feelings. Cindy agrees. It just seems too risky.

On Sunday night, I e-mail Pastor Nixon. "Dear John," I write, "I think the last couple weeks have probably been helpful for everyone in getting a feel for the future of Connect. . . . My sense at this point is that, with all the moving parts, it probably wouldn't be best for me to have an overall leadership role." As I hit send, I feel heavyhearted. This is very, very hard for me. I'm letting go of something I feel excited about. Years earlier I probably would have tried to make this work. But not this time. Resigned, I go to bed.

The next morning, I wake up before dawn. Some words are tumbling over and over in my head: *Walk in the fullness of God's blessings.* The words are familiar. They're the words Debi had used when she'd left the strange message on my answering machine a week earlier. *Walk in the fullness of God's blessings.*

I wander downstairs and sit for a while in our overstuffed chair. On the end table beside me is my Bible. I grab it and flip to the concordance to see if there's an entry with the words *fullness of God's blessings.* The closest thing is a single entry for "fullness of God." It's in Ephesians 3:19, "That you may be filled to the measure of all the fullness of God." That's interesting. Ephesians was the book that affected me so powerfully when I'd read through Scripture several months before. I look up the word *walk.* Two of the entries are from Ephesians—Ephesians 4:17 and 5:8. In fact, all three of these verses are from the passage in the heart of Ephesians about taking the Christian walk seriously—making the most of our time.

I sit quietly in the chair. How strange that I should wake up with these words in my head—and that they should be so heavily from Ephesians. And the final word *blessings*—Ephesians is bursting with this word from the very start. I reflect on the message from Debi—this strange and spiritual phone message in the middle of this murky decision-making process. Seventeen years since I've seen her, and she's calling because she feels like God asked her to. She's praying that I will "walk in the fullness of God's blessings" and says maybe that means something to me. Sitting there alone, I shake my head. I'm tired of getting my hopes dashed, tired of looking for meaning when maybe there isn't any. I don't want this to be another one of those times. As I leave for work, I don't say anything about this to Cindy.

Later that morning, I get a reply to my e-mail from Pastor Nixon. "Andy," he writes, "please don't decide yet on any limitations." The pastors want Cindy and me to meet again with them—and with the leadership team as well. Both groups have things to clarify and resolve; the former angst is replaced by healing. With a newfound peace, they invite Cindy and me to lead this worship community—to work in ministry together.

*****

At Christmastime our family of five is introduced to the church. For the message, I speak on Isaiah 7—the sign of Immanuel. The message, titled "Christmas Is About Receiving," is about humbly submitting to God's plans, not pushing our own. I know something about this.

To close the message, I had needed a good story, and I remembered one we had published years before in *The Front Porch*. It was called "Our Christmas

Angels" by a freelance writer named Susan Farr Fahncke. Susan told of being a single mom going through an especially tough time at Christmas. I had always loved this story. At the close of my talk, I read it aloud.

It was December 23rd. Christmas looked bleak to me—a single mom trying to get through college while raising two children. I looked around, realization spreading over me like a slow, twisting pain. We were poor.

Our tiny house contained two bedrooms, so small that my daughter's crib barely fit into one, and my son's twin bed and dresser filled the other. I made my bed every night on the living room floor. We felt snug, only a few feet from each other—day and night. We all experienced a sense of security and closeness that we would not have known in other circumstances.

The snow fell softly, silently. At a quarter to eleven, I wrapped myself in a blanket and sat down to watch the powdery flakes flutter in the moonlight. Suddenly, my front door vibrated under a pounding fist.

Alarmed, I wondered who would visit me so late at night. I cautiously opened the door and found several strangers grinning from ear to ear, their arms laden with boxes and bags.

Confused, but finding their joy contagious, I grinned back.

"Are you Susan?" The man stepped forward, pushing a box at me.

Nodding stupidly, unable to find my voice, I was sure they thought me mentally deficient.

"These are for you." The woman thrust another box at me with a beaming smile. The porch light reflecting on the falling snow cast a glow on her dark hair, lending her an angelic appearance.

I looked down into her box, which overflowed with treats, a fat turkey, and all the makings of a traditional Christmas dinner. My eyes filled with tears.

I finally found my voice and invited them in. Following the husband, two children staggered under the weight of their boxes. The family introduced themselves to me, and told me they brought these packages for my children and me. This wonderful family, total strangers to me, somehow knew exactly what we needed. They brought wrapped gifts for each of us, a full buffet, and many extras I could never afford. Visions of a beautiful, normal Christmas literally danced in my head. Somehow my secret wish for Christmas had materialized right in front of me. Someone heard the desperate prayers of a mother, and He sent His angels my way.

My mysterious angels handed me a white envelope, gave me another round of grins, and hugged me. They wished me a Merry Christmas and disappeared into the night as quickly as they appeared.

Amazed and deeply touched, I looked around me at the boxes and gifts strewn at my feet and felt the ache of depression transformed into childlike joy. I began to cry. I sobbed tears of deepest gratitude. A sense of peace filled me as God's love enveloped me like a warm quilt. Heart-filled, I dropped to my knees amid the boxes and offered a prayer of thanks.

Rising, I wrapped the blanket around me and sat down at the window again. Then I remembered the envelope. Ripping it open, I gasped. A shower of bills flitted to the floor. Gathering them up, I began to count the fives, tens, and twenties. My vision blurred with tears as I counted and recounted. Sobbing again, I said aloud, "One hundred dollars."

In addition to showering me with gifts, my angels understood how desperately I needed money. They couldn't have known it, but I had received a disconnect notice from the gas company. I simply didn't have the money to pay and feared my family would be without heat for Christmas. The envelope of cash would provide warmth and a tree. We had all we needed and more.

I looked at my children, sleeping soundly, and through my tears I smiled my first carefree smile in months. My smile turned to a grin as I though[t] about tomorrow—Christmas Eve. One visit from complete strangers magically changed a painful day into [a] special one we would always remember.

Several years have passed since our Christmas angels visited. In that time, I remarried and my little family has been richly blessed. Each year, we choose a family less blessed than we are. We bring them carefully selected gifts, food, treats, and as much money as we can spare—our way of passing on the gift given to us. We hope that some day the families we share with will also pass it on.

Wherever my angels are, I thank you. And so do many other families. God bless you and all the other Christmas angels out there.[1]

By the end of the story, I feel emotional. I remember well what the dark nights felt like—the deep emptiness and confusion of it all. I remember the many knocks on the door—how hopeful they felt. But not only this. Here I am, using a story from my old dream in my new dream. Where I had previously been more concerned about filling my nets with fish, here I am entrusted with the privilege of feeding sheep. By learning to delight myself in the Lord, He has given me the desires of my heart.

* * * * *

In the publishing business, there's a term called *reprint rights.* When a publisher wants to reprint a story that's already been printed, read, and then discarded, the publisher purchases the rights from the author of the story. It's not common for reprint rights to be purchased; the publisher has to see enough value in the author's story. When it does happen, the author's story is, in a sense, given a new life.

On this morning in December, that's a little how I feel.

1. "Our Christmas Angels," reprinted with permission of Susan Farr Fahncke at www.2theheart.com.

# Epilogue

When this experience began, I thought that stepping out in faith was supposed to be exciting. I now think that stepping in faith is supposed to be painful. Faith is painful because it means that we're releasing our human grip, that we're believing what we don't see, that we're entrusting God with control of our lives. Our flesh shudders against this, but our spirit knows it's the only way to live.

Many of us are willing to take risks in other areas of life—but not in the realm of faith. I've learned that it should be the opposite. We should be cautious in other areas of life so that we're not consumed by them—so that we're not kneeling at their altars, praying that things will work out. There's nothing wrong with reputable pursuits, just as there's nothing wrong with fishing. But when these become too important to us—when our feelings toward them come dangerously close to worship—then we've got to pull back and recalibrate. This is the story of Simon Peter—the story of all who want to follow Christ.

In the same way that Christ repeatedly met Peter in the context of fishing, He meets each of us where our natural passions and interests lie. I believe that the Lord met me on the sea of publishing—that He gave me a dream for a publication that celebrated the beauty of ordinary people. And it was a good dream. The motto for *The Front Porch* was "Where people share life," and it was a true honor to see hundreds of stories pouring in each week from people who wanted to share their lives. But at some point for me, the dream became too important. It consumed too much of *my* life. It became a god—and God doesn't give us other gods.

This is *The Front Porch*'s final story: my sharing this experience and all that went with it. I don't fully understand all that happened, and frankly, I would never want to go through it again. But I'm glad for the sifting I've been through—glad that apparently I had enough grain of faith remaining to be called to discipleship. Still, I recognize that on this side of the sea of glass, the battle for the soul isn't over for any of us. We can take comfort that Peter, too, would continue to need an occasional nudge in the right direction. Indeed, that's the life story we all share, no matter what age we might be.

This past spring I was walking through our house when my five-year-old, Summer, called out to me from our living room.

Daddy, come here! she said. I want to show you something!

I came around the corner to see Summer playing a children's computer game called ice fishing. She looked absolutely delighted. One by one she was reeling in large yellow fish.

Look at all the fish I'm catching! she screamed.

The words had a familiar ring to them.

# Acknowledgments

To Cindy: You're the best thing that's ever happened to me. I love you.

To Ally, Morgan, and Summer: You light up our lives. Mommy and I love you so much.

To Dad, Mom, and Angel: Wherever we were together was my favorite place in the world.

To Charles and Evelyn Griffin: Thanks for your love during a difficult time. I understand how it feels to want a hurting daughter close by.

To Chris Blake, Mark Smith, Jill Aalborg Payne, Pauline Deeb Bulima, Jackie Smith, Amanda Sauder Maggard, Jeff and Kay Dever, Chris Komisar, Debra LoGuercio, and many others: Thanks for some memorable days working together.

To Joe, Karen, and David: Thank you.

To Jake and Ella: Thank you.

To Cliff Goldstein, Jeff Emde, Paul Carpenter, Ron and Stephanie Mahlo, Lynn Sauls, Jeannette Johnson, Todd Chobotar, and others: Thanks for being there.

To Mr. Turk: Thanks for all the talks.

To early readers of this manuscript—Gerald Shapiro, Joy Castro, Robert Brooke, Gary Krause, Chris Blake, Lynn Sauls, Marcel Schwantes, Bernie Anderson, Alex Bryan: Thanks for making it better.

To dear friends and mentors—William Johnsson, David Smith, George Gibson, Frank Lalli, Wilma McClarty, Greg Rumsey, John Nixon, and all their colleagues: Thanks for your support and confidence.

To Pacific Press: Thank you.

To our church family: It has been the highest possible privilege.